Gifts to Charities – net cost for indiv…

(a) By covenants by indivi…

or (b) By deduction from…

Gross amount received by Charity	Net cost to Donor Top rate of income tax		Gross amount received by Charity	Net cost to Donor Top rate of income tax	
£	25% £	40% £	£	25% £	40% £
1	0·75	0·60	51	38·25	30·60
2	1·50	1·20	52	39·00	31·20
3	2·25	1·80	53	39·75	31·80
4	3·00	2·40	54	40·50	32·40
5	3·75	3·00	55	41·25	33·00
6	4·50	3·60	56	42·00	33·60
7	5·25	4·20	57	42·75	34·20
8	6·00	4·80	58	43·50	34·80
9	6·75	5·40	59	44·25	35·40
10	7·50	6·00	60	45·00	36·00
11	8·25	6·60	61	45·75	36·60
12	9·00	7·20	62	46·50	37·20
13	9·75	7·80	63	47·25	37·80
14	10·50	8·40	64	48·00	38·40
15	11·25	9·00	65	48·75	39·00
16	12·00	9·60	66	49·50	39·60
17	12·75	10·20	67	50·25	40·20
18	13·50	10·80	68	51·00	40·80
19	14·25	11·40	69	51·75	41·40
20	15·00	12·00	70	52·50	42·00
21	15·75	12·60	71	53·25	42·60
22	16·50	13·20	72	54·00	43·20
23	17·25	13·80	73	54·75	43·80
24	18·00	14·40	74	55·50	44·40
25	18·75	15·00	75	56·25	45·00
26	19·50	15·60	76	57·00	45·60
27	20·25	16·20	77	57·75	46·20
28	21·00	16·80	78	58·50	46·80
29	21·75	17·40	79	59·25	47·40
30	22·50	18·00	80	60·00	48·00
31	23·25	18·60	81	60·75	48·60
32	24·00	19·20	82	61·50	49·20
33	24·75	19·80	83	62·25	49·80
34	25·50	20·40	84	63·00	50·40
35	26·25	21·00	85	63·75	51·00
36	27·00	21·60	86	64·50	51·60
37	27·75	22·20	87	65·25	52·20
38	28·50	22·80	88	66·00	52·80
39	29·25	23·40	89	66·75	53·40
40	30·00	24·00	90	67·50	54·00
41	30·75	24·60	91	68·25	54·60
42	31·50	25·20	92	69·00	55·20
43	32·25	25·80	93	69·75	55·80
44	33·00	26·40	94	70·50	56·40
45	33·75	27·00	95	71·25	57·00
46	34·50	27·60	96	72·00	57·60
47	35·25	28·20	97	72·75	58·20
48	36·00	28·80	98	73·50	58·80
49	36·75	29·40	99	74·25	59·40
50	37·50	30·00	100	75·00	60·00

Net cost to Donor	Gross amount received by Charity, if Donor's top rate of income tax		Donor	Gross amount received by Charity, if Donor's top rate of income tax	
£	25% £	40% £	£	25% £	40% £
1	1·33	1·67	51	68·00	85·00
2	2·67	3·33	52	69·33	86·67
3	4·00	5·00	53	70·67	88·33
4	5·33	6·67	54	72·00	90·00
5	6·67	8·33	55	73·33	91·67
6	8·00	10·00	56	74·67	93·33
7	9·33	11·67	57	76·00	95·00
8	10·67	13·33	58	77·33	96·67
9	12·00	15·00	59	78·67	98·33
10	13·33	16·67	60	80·00	100·00
11	14·67	18·33	61	81·33	101·67
12	16·00	20·00	62	82·67	103·33
13	17·33	21·67	63	84·00	105·00
14	18·67	23·33	64	85·33	106·67
15	20·00	25·00	65	86·67	108·33
16	21·33	26·67	66	88·00	110·00
17	22·67	28·33	67	89·33	111·67
18	24·00	30·00	68	90·67	113·33
19	25·33	31·67	69	92·00	115·00
20	26·67	33·33	70	93·33	116·67
21	28·00	35·00	71	94·67	118·33
22	29·33	36·67	72	96·00	120·00
23	30·67	38·33	73	97·33	121·67
24	32·00	40·00	74	98·67	123·33
25	33·33	41·67	75	100·00	125·00
26	34·67	43·33	76	101·33	126·67
27	36·00	45·00	77	102·67	128·33
28	37·33	46·67	78	104·00	130·00
29	38·67	48·33	79	105·33	131·67
30	40·00	50·00	80	106·67	133·33
31	41·33	51·67	81	108·00	135·00
32	42·67	53·33	82	109·33	136·67
33	44·00	55·00	83	110·67	138·33
34	45·33	56·67	84	112·00	140·00
35	46·67	58·33	85	113·33	141·67
36	48·00	60·00	86	114·67	143·33
37	49·33	61·67	87	116·00	145·00
38	50·67	63·33	88	117·33	146·67
39	52·00	65·00	89	118·67	148·33
40	53·33	66·67	90	120·00	150·00
41	54·67	68·33	91	121·33	151·67
42	56·00	70·00	92	122·67	153·33
43	57·33	71·67	93	124·00	155·00
44	58·67	73·33	94	125·33	156·67
45	60·00	75·00	95	126·67	158·33
46	61·33	76·67	96	128·00	160·00
47	62·67	78·33	97	129·33	161·67
48	64·00	80·00	98	130·67	163·33
49	65·33	81·67	99	132·00	165·00
50	66·67	83·33	100	133·33	166·67

20% Income Tax Lower Rate 1994/95 (a)
Capital Gains Tax Lower Rate 1994/95 (b)

a) Payable on first £3,000 of taxable income
b) Payable on first slice of chargeable gain over £5,800
where taxable income is less than £3,000

£ or p	Tax £ or p	£ or p	Tax £ or p	£	Tax £	£	Tax £	£	Tax £	£	Tax £	£	Tax £	£	Tax £	£	Tax £	£	Tax £
1	0·20	51	10·20	101	20·20	151	30·20	201	40·20	251	50·20	301	60·20	351	70·20	401	80·20	451	90·20
2	0·40	52	10·40	102	20·40	152	30·40	202	40·40	252	50·40	302	60·40	352	70·40	402	80·40	452	90·40
3	0·60	53	10·60	103	20·60	153	30·60	203	40·60	253	50·60	303	60·60	353	70·60	403	80·60	453	90·60
4	0·80	54	10·80	104	20·80	154	30·80	204	40·80	254	50·80	304	60·80	354	70·80	404	80·80	454	90·80
5	1·00	55	11·00	105	21·00	155	31·00	205	41·00	255	51·00	305	61·00	355	71·00	405	81·00	455	91·00
6	1·20	56	11·20	106	21·20	156	31·20	206	41·20	256	51·20	306	61·20	356	71·20	406	81·20	456	91·20
7	1·40	57	11·40	107	21·40	157	31·40	207	41·40	257	51·40	307	61·40	357	71·40	407	81·40	457	91·40
8	1·60	58	11·60	108	21·60	158	31·60	208	41·60	258	51·60	308	61·60	358	71·60	408	81·60	458	91·60
9	1·80	59	11·80	109	21·80	159	31·80	209	41·80	259	51·80	309	61·80	359	71·80	409	81·80	459	91·80
10	2·00	60	12·00	110	22·00	160	32·00	210	42·00	260	52·00	310	62·00	360	72·00	410	82·00	460	92·00
11	2·20	61	12·20	111	22·20	161	32·20	211	42·20	261	52·20	311	62·20	361	72·20	411	82·20	461	92·20
12	2·40	62	12·40	112	22·40	162	32·40	212	42·40	262	52·40	312	62·40	362	72·40	412	82·40	462	92·40
13	2·60	63	12·60	113	22·60	163	32·60	213	42·60	263	52·60	313	62·60	363	72·60	413	82·60	463	92·60
14	2·80	64	12·80	114	22·80	164	32·80	214	42·80	264	52·80	314	62·80	364	72·80	414	82·80	464	92·80
15	3·00	65	13·00	115	23·00	165	33·00	215	43·00	265	53·00	315	63·00	365	73·00	415	83·00	465	93·00
16	3·20	66	13·20	116	23·20	166	33·20	216	43·20	266	53·20	316	63·20	366	73·20	416	83·20	466	93·20
17	3·40	67	13·40	117	23·40	167	33·40	217	43·40	267	53·40	317	63·40	367	73·40	417	83·40	467	93·40
18	3·60	68	13·60	118	23·60	168	33·60	218	43·60	268	53·60	318	63·60	368	73·60	418	83·60	468	93·60
19	3·80	69	13·80	119	23·80	169	33·80	219	43·80	269	53·80	319	63·80	369	73·80	419	83·80	469	93·80
20	4·00	70	14·00	120	24·00	170	34·00	220	44·00	270	54·00	320	64·00	370	74·00	420	84·00	470	94·00
21	4·20	71	14·20	121	24·20	171	34·20	221	44·20	271	54·20	321	64·20	371	74·20	421	84·20	471	94·20
22	4·40	72	14·40	122	24·40	172	34·40	222	44·40	272	54·40	322	64·40	372	74·40	422	84·40	472	94·40
23	4·60	73	14·60	123	24·60	173	34·60	223	44·60	273	54·60	323	64·60	373	74·60	423	84·60	473	94·60
24	4·80	74	14·80	124	24·80	174	34·80	224	44·80	274	54·80	324	64·80	374	74·80	424	84·80	474	94·80
25	5·00	75	15·00	125	25·00	175	35·00	225	45·00	275	55·00	325	65·00	375	75·00	425	85·00	475	95·00
26	5·20	76	15·20	126	25·20	176	35·20	226	45·20	276	55·20	326	65·20	376	75·20	426	85·20	476	95·20
27	5·40	77	15·40	127	25·40	177	35·40	227	45·40	277	55·40	327	65·40	377	75·40	427	85·40	477	95·40
28	5·60	78	15·60	128	25·60	178	35·60	228	45·60	278	55·60	328	65·60	378	75·60	428	85·60	478	95·60
29	5·80	79	15·80	129	25·80	179	35·80	229	45·80	279	55·80	329	65·80	379	75·80	429	85·80	479	95·80
30	6·00	80	16·00	130	26·00	180	36·00	230	46·00	280	56·00	330	66·00	380	76·00	430	86·00	480	96·00
31	6·20	81	16·20	131	26·20	181	36·20	231	46·20	281	56·20	331	66·20	381	76·20	431	86·20	481	96·20
32	6·40	82	16·40	132	26·40	182	36·40	232	46·40	282	56·40	332	66·40	382	76·40	432	86·40	482	96·40
33	6·60	83	16·60	133	26·60	183	36·60	233	46·60	283	56·60	333	66·60	383	76·60	433	86·60	483	96·60
34	6·80	84	16·80	134	26·80	184	36·80	234	46·80	284	56·80	334	66·80	384	76·80	434	86·80	484	96·80
35	7·00	85	17·00	135	27·00	185	37·00	235	47·00	285	57·00	335	67·00	385	77·00	435	87·00	485	97·00
36	7·20	86	17·20	136	27·20	186	37·20	236	47·20	286	57·20	336	67·20	386	77·20	436	87·20	486	97·20
37	7·40	87	17·40	137	27·40	187	37·40	237	47·40	287	57·40	337	67·40	387	77·40	437	87·40	487	97·40
38	7·60	88	17·60	138	27·60	188	37·60	238	47·60	288	57·60	338	67·60	388	77·60	438	87·60	488	97·60
39	7·80	89	17·80	139	27·80	189	37·80	239	47·80	289	57·80	339	67·80	389	77·80	439	87·80	489	97·80
40	8·00	90	18·00	140	28·00	190	38·00	240	48·00	290	58·00	340	68·00	390	78·00	440	88·00	490	98·00
41	8·20	91	18·20	141	28·20	191	38·20	241	48·20	291	58·20	341	68·20	391	78·20	441	88·20	491	98·20
42	8·40	92	18·40	142	28·40	192	38·40	242	48·40	292	58·40	342	68·40	392	78·40	442	88·40	492	98·40
43	8·60	93	18·60	143	28·60	193	38·60	243	48·60	293	58·60	343	68·60	393	78·60	443	88·60	493	98·60
44	8·80	94	18·80	144	28·80	194	38·80	244	48·80	294	58·80	344	68·80	394	78·80	444	88·80	494	98·80
45	9·00	95	19·00	145	29·00	195	39·00	245	49·00	295	59·00	345	69·00	395	79·00	445	89·00	495	99·00
46	9·20	96	19·20	146	29·20	196	39·20	246	49·20	296	59·20	346	69·20	396	79·20	446	89·20	496	99·20
47	9·40	97	19·40	147	29·40	197	39·40	247	49·40	297	59·40	347	69·40	397	79·40	447	89·40	497	99·40
48	9·60	98	19·60	148	29·60	198	39·60	248	49·60	298	59·60	348	69·60	398	79·60	448	89·60	498	99·60
49	9·80	99	19·80	149	29·80	199	39·80	249	49·80	299	59·80	349	69·80	399	79·80	449	89·80	499	99·80
50	10·00	100	20·00	150	30·00	200	40·00	250	50·00	300	60·00	350	70·00	400	80·00	450	90·00	500	100·00

On Tax	£1,000 £200	£1,500 £300	£2,000 £400	£2,500 £500	£3,000 £600

a) Payable on first £3,000 of taxable income
b) Payable on first slice of chargeable gain over £5,800
where taxable income is less than £3,000

Income Tax Lower Rate 1994/95 (a)   20%
Capital Gains Tax Lower Rate 1994/95 (b)

£	Tax £	£	Tax £	£	Tax £	£	Tax £	£	Tax £	£	Tax £	£	Tax £	£	Tax £	£	Tax £	£	Tax £
501	100·20	551	110·20	601	120·20	651	130·20	701	140·20	751	150·20	801	160·20	851	170·20	901	180·20	951	190·20
502	100·40	552	110·40	602	120·40	652	130·40	702	140·40	752	150·40	802	160·40	852	170·40	902	180·40	952	190·40
503	100·60	553	110·60	603	120·60	653	130·60	703	140·60	753	150·60	803	160·60	853	170·60	903	180·60	953	190·60
504	100·80	554	110·80	604	120·80	654	130·80	704	140·80	754	150·80	804	160·80	854	170·80	904	180·80	954	190·80
505	101·00	555	111·00	605	121·00	655	131·00	705	141·00	755	151·00	805	161·00	855	171·00	905	181·00	955	191·00
506	101·20	556	111·20	606	121·20	656	131·20	706	141·20	756	151·20	806	161·20	856	171·20	906	181·20	956	191·20
507	101·40	557	111·40	607	121·40	657	131·40	707	141·40	757	151·40	807	161·40	857	171·40	907	181·40	957	191·40
508	101·60	558	111·60	608	121·60	658	131·60	708	141·60	758	151·60	808	161·60	858	171·60	908	181·60	958	191·60
509	101·80	559	111·80	609	121·80	659	131·80	709	141·80	759	151·80	809	161·80	859	171·80	909	181·80	959	191·80
510	102·00	560	112·00	610	122·00	660	132·00	710	142·00	760	152·00	810	162·00	860	172·00	910	182·00	960	192·00
511	102·20	561	112·20	611	122·20	661	132·20	711	142·20	761	152·20	811	162·20	861	172·20	911	182·20	961	192·20
512	102·40	562	112·40	612	122·40	662	132·40	712	142·40	762	152·40	812	162·40	862	172·40	912	182·40	962	192·40
513	102·60	563	112·60	613	122·60	663	132·60	713	142·60	763	152·60	813	162·60	863	172·60	913	182·60	963	192·60
514	102·80	564	112·80	614	122·80	664	132·80	714	142·80	764	152·80	814	162·80	864	172·80	914	182·80	964	192·80
515	103·00	565	113·00	615	123·00	665	133·00	715	143·00	765	153·00	815	163·00	865	173·00	915	183·00	965	193·00
516	103·20	566	113·20	616	123·20	666	133·20	716	143·20	766	153·20	816	163·20	866	173·20	916	183·20	966	193·20
517	103·40	567	113·40	617	123·40	667	133·40	717	143·40	767	153·40	817	163·40	867	173·40	917	183·40	967	193·40
518	103·60	568	113·60	618	123·60	668	133·60	718	143·60	768	153·60	818	163·60	868	173·60	918	183·60	968	193·60
519	103·80	569	113·80	619	123·80	669	133·80	719	143·80	769	153·80	819	163·80	869	173·80	919	183·80	969	193·80
520	104·00	570	114·00	620	124·00	670	134·00	720	144·00	770	154·00	820	164·00	870	174·00	920	184·00	970	194·00
521	104·20	571	114·20	621	124·20	671	134·20	721	144·20	771	154·20	821	164·20	871	174·20	921	184·20	971	194·20
522	104·40	572	114·40	622	124·40	672	134·40	722	144·40	772	154·40	822	164·40	872	174·40	922	184·40	972	194·40
523	104·60	573	114·60	623	124·60	673	134·60	723	144·60	773	154·60	823	164·60	873	174·60	923	184·60	973	194·60
524	104·80	574	114·80	624	124·80	674	134·80	724	144·80	774	154·80	824	164·80	874	174·80	924	184·80	974	194·80
525	105·00	575	115·00	625	125·00	675	135·00	725	145·00	775	155·00	825	165·00	875	175·00	925	185·00	975	195·00
526	105·20	576	115·20	626	125·20	676	135·20	726	145·20	776	155·20	826	165·20	876	175·20	926	185·20	976	195·20
527	105·40	577	115·40	627	125·40	677	135·40	727	145·40	777	155·40	827	165·40	877	175·40	927	185·40	977	195·40
528	105·60	578	115·60	628	125·60	678	135·60	728	145·60	778	155·60	828	165·60	878	175·60	928	185·60	978	195·60
529	105·80	579	115·80	629	125·80	679	135·80	729	145·80	779	155·80	829	165·80	879	175·80	929	185·80	979	195·80
530	106·00	580	116·00	630	126·00	680	136·00	730	146·00	780	156·00	830	166·00	880	176·00	930	186·00	980	196·00
531	106·20	581	116·20	631	126·20	681	136·20	731	146·20	781	156·20	831	166·20	881	176·20	931	186·20	981	196·20
532	106·40	582	116·40	632	126·40	682	136·40	732	146·40	782	156·40	832	166·40	882	176·40	932	186·40	982	196·40
533	106·60	583	116·60	633	126·60	683	136·60	733	146·60	783	156·60	833	166·60	883	176·60	933	186·60	983	196·60
534	106·80	584	116·80	634	126·80	684	136·80	734	146·80	784	156·80	834	166·80	884	176·80	934	186·80	984	196·80
535	107·00	585	117·00	635	127·00	685	137·00	735	147·00	785	157·00	835	167·00	885	177·00	935	187·00	985	197·00
536	107·20	586	117·20	636	127·20	686	137·20	736	147·20	786	157·20	836	167·20	886	177·20	936	187·20	986	197·20
537	107·40	587	117·40	637	127·40	687	137·40	737	147·40	787	157·40	837	167·40	887	177·40	937	187·40	987	197·40
538	107·60	588	117·60	638	127·60	688	137·60	738	147·60	788	157·60	838	167·60	888	177·60	938	187·60	988	197·60
539	107·80	589	117·80	639	127·80	689	137·80	739	147·80	789	157·80	839	167·80	889	177·80	939	187·80	989	197·80
540	108·00	590	118·00	640	128·00	690	138·00	740	148·00	790	158·00	840	168·00	890	178·00	940	188·00	990	198·00
541	108·20	591	118·20	641	128·20	691	138·20	741	148·20	791	158·20	841	168·20	891	178·20	941	188·20	991	198·20
542	108·40	592	118·40	642	128·40	692	138·40	742	148·40	792	158·40	842	168·40	892	178·40	942	188·40	992	198·40
543	108·60	593	118·60	643	128·60	693	138·60	743	148·60	793	158·60	843	168·60	893	178·60	943	188·60	993	198·60
544	108·80	594	118·80	644	128·80	694	138·80	744	148·80	794	158·80	844	168·80	894	178·80	944	188·80	994	198·80
545	109·00	595	119·00	645	129·00	695	139·00	745	149·00	795	159·00	845	169·00	895	179·00	945	189·00	995	199·00
546	109·20	596	119·20	646	129·20	696	139·20	746	149·20	796	159·20	846	169·20	896	179·20	946	189·20	996	199·20
547	109·40	597	119·40	647	129·40	697	139·40	747	149·40	797	159·40	847	169·40	897	179·40	947	189·40	997	199·40
548	109·60	598	119·60	648	129·60	698	139·60	748	149·60	798	159·60	848	169·60	898	179·60	948	189·60	998	199·60
549	109·80	599	119·80	649	129·80	699	139·80	749	149·80	799	159·80	849	169·80	899	179·80	949	189·80	999	199·80
550	110·00	600	120·00	650	130·00	700	140·00	750	150·00	800	160·00	850	170·00	900	180·00	950	190·00	1,000	200·00

25% Income Tax Basic Rate 1988/89 to 1994/95 Capital Gains Tax Basic Rate 1988/89 to 1994/9

Corporation Tax: Rate for Companies with Small Profits: F.Y. 1988 to 1994

£ or p	Tax £ or p	£ or p	Tax £ or p	£	Tax £	£	Tax £	£	Tax £	£	Tax £	£	Tax £	£	Tax £	£	Tax £	£	Tax £
1	0·25	51	12·75	101	25·25	151	37·75	201	50·25	251	62·75	301	75·25	351	87·75	401	100·25	451	112·75
2	0·50	52	13·00	102	25·50	152	38·00	202	50·50	252	63·00	302	75·50	352	88·00	402	100·50	452	113·00
3	0·75	53	13·25	103	25·75	153	38·25	203	50·75	253	63·25	303	75·75	353	88·25	403	100·75	453	113·25
4	1·00	54	13·50	104	26·00	154	38·50	204	51·00	254	63·50	304	76·00	354	88·50	404	101·00	454	113·50
5	1·25	55	13·75	105	26·25	155	38·75	205	51·25	255	63·75	305	76·25	355	88·75	405	101·25	455	113·75
6	1·50	56	14·00	106	26·50	156	39·00	206	51·50	256	64·00	306	76·50	356	89·00	406	101·50	456	114·00
7	1·75	57	14·25	107	26·75	157	39·25	207	51·75	257	64·25	307	76·75	357	89·25	407	101·75	457	114·25
8	2·00	58	14·50	108	27·00	158	39·50	208	52·00	258	64·50	308	77·00	358	89·50	408	102·00	458	114·50
9	2·25	59	14·75	109	27·25	159	39·75	209	52·25	259	64·75	309	77·25	359	89·75	409	102·25	459	114·75
10	2·50	60	15·00	110	27·50	160	40·00	210	52·50	260	65·00	310	77·50	360	90·00	410	102·50	460	115·00
11	2·75	61	15·25	111	27·75	161	40·25	211	52·75	261	65·25	311	77·75	361	90·25	411	102·75	461	115·25
12	3·00	62	15·50	112	28·00	162	40·50	212	53·00	262	65·50	312	78·00	362	90·50	412	103·00	462	115·50
13	3·25	63	15·75	113	28·25	163	40·75	213	53·25	263	65·75	313	78·25	363	90·75	413	103·25	463	115·75
14	3·50	64	16·00	114	28·50	164	41·00	214	53·50	264	66·00	314	78·50	364	91·00	414	103·50	464	116·00
15	3·75	65	16·25	115	28·75	165	41·25	215	53·75	265	66·25	315	78·75	365	91·25	415	103·75	465	116·25
16	4·00	66	16·50	116	29·00	166	41·50	216	54·00	266	66·50	316	79·00	366	91·50	416	104·00	466	116·50
17	4·25	67	16·75	117	29·25	167	41·75	217	54·25	267	66·75	317	79·25	367	91·75	417	104·25	467	116·75
18	4·50	68	17·00	118	29·50	168	42·00	218	54·50	268	67·00	318	79·50	368	92·00	418	104·50	468	117·00
19	4·75	69	17·25	119	29·75	169	42·25	219	54·75	269	67·25	319	79·75	369	92·25	419	104·75	469	117·25
20	5·00	70	17·50	120	30·00	170	42·50	220	55·00	270	67·50	320	80·00	370	92·50	420	105·00	470	117·50
21	5·25	71	17·75	121	30·25	171	42·75	221	55·25	271	67·75	321	80·25	371	92·75	421	105·25	471	117·75
22	5·50	72	18·00	122	30·50	172	43·00	222	55·50	272	68·00	322	80·50	372	93·00	422	105·50	472	118·00
23	5·75	73	18·25	123	30·75	173	43·25	223	55·75	273	68·25	323	80·75	373	93·25	423	105·75	473	118·25
24	6·00	74	18·50	124	31·00	174	43·50	224	56·00	274	68·50	324	81·00	374	93·50	424	106·00	474	118·50
25	6·25	75	18·75	125	31·25	175	43·75	225	56·25	275	68·75	325	81·25	375	93·75	425	106·25	475	118·75
26	6·50	76	19·00	126	31·50	176	44·00	226	56·50	276	69·00	326	81·50	376	94·00	426	106·50	476	119·00
27	6·75	77	19·25	127	31·75	177	44·25	227	56·75	277	69·25	327	81·75	377	94·25	427	106·75	477	119·25
28	7·00	78	19·50	128	32·00	178	44·50	228	57·00	278	69·50	328	82·00	378	94·50	428	107·00	478	119·50
29	7·25	79	19·75	129	32·25	179	44·75	229	57·25	279	69·75	329	82·25	379	94·75	429	107·25	479	119·75
30	7·50	80	20·00	130	32·50	180	45·00	230	57·50	280	70·00	330	82·50	380	95·00	430	107·50	480	120·00
31	7·75	81	20·25	131	32·75	181	45·25	231	57·75	281	70·25	331	82·75	381	95·25	431	107·75	481	120·25
32	8·00	82	20·50	132	33·00	182	45·50	232	58·00	282	70·50	332	83·00	382	95·50	432	108·00	482	120·50
33	8·25	83	20·75	133	33·25	183	45·75	233	58·25	283	70·75	333	83·25	383	95·75	433	108·25	483	120·75
34	8·50	84	21·00	134	33·50	184	46·00	234	58·50	284	71·00	334	83·50	384	96·00	434	108·50	484	121·00
35	8·75	85	21·25	135	33·75	185	46·25	235	58·75	285	71·25	335	83·75	385	96·25	435	108·75	485	121·25
36	9·00	86	21·50	136	34·00	186	46·50	236	59·00	286	71·50	336	84·00	386	96·50	436	109·00	486	121·50
37	9·25	87	21·75	137	34·25	187	46·75	237	59·25	287	71·75	337	84·25	387	96·75	437	109·25	487	121·75
38	9·50	88	22·00	138	34·50	188	47·00	238	59·50	288	72·00	338	84·50	388	97·00	438	109·50	488	122·00
39	9·75	89	22·25	139	34·75	189	47·25	239	59·75	289	72·25	339	84·75	389	97·25	439	109·75	489	122·25
40	10·00	90	22·50	140	35·00	190	47·50	240	60·00	290	72·50	340	85·00	390	97·50	440	110·00	490	122·50
41	10·25	91	22·75	141	35·25	191	47·75	241	60·25	291	72·75	341	85·25	391	97·75	441	110·25	491	122·75
42	10·50	92	23·00	142	35·50	192	48·00	242	60·50	292	73·00	342	85·50	392	98·00	442	110·50	492	123·00
43	10·75	93	23·25	143	35·75	193	48·25	243	60·75	293	73·25	343	85·75	393	98·25	443	110·75	493	123·25
44	11·00	94	23·50	144	36·00	194	48·50	244	61·00	294	73·50	344	86·00	394	98·50	444	111·00	494	123·50
45	11·25	95	23·75	145	36·25	195	48·75	245	61·25	295	73·75	345	86·25	395	98·75	445	111·25	495	123·75
46	11·50	96	24·00	146	36·50	196	49·00	246	61·50	296	74·00	346	86·50	396	99·00	446	111·50	496	124·00
47	11·75	97	24·25	147	36·75	197	49·25	247	61·75	297	74·25	347	86·75	397	99·25	447	111·75	497	124·25
48	12·00	98	24·50	148	37·00	198	49·50	248	62·00	298	74·50	348	87·00	398	99·50	448	112·00	498	124·50
49	12·25	99	24·75	149	37·25	199	49·75	249	62·25	299	74·75	349	87·25	399	99·75	449	112·25	499	124·75
50	12·50	100	25·00	150	37·50	200	50·00	250	62·50	300	75·00	350	87·50	400	100·00	450	112·50	500	125·00

| | On Tax | £1,000 £250 | | £1,500 £375 | | £2,000 £500 | | £2,500 £625 | | £3,000 £750 | | £3,500 £875 | | £4,000 £1,000 | | £4,500 £1,125 | | £5,000 £1,250 | |

ncome Tax Basic Rate 1988/89 to 1994/95   Capital Gains Tax Basic Rate 1988/89 to 1994/95   25%
Corporation Tax: Rate for Companies with Small Profits: F.Y. 1988 to 1994

£	Tax £	£	Tax £	£	Tax £	£	Tax £	£	Tax £	£	Tax £	£	Tax £	£	Tax £	£	Tax £	£	Tax £
501	125.25	551	137.75	601	150.25	651	162.75	701	175.25	751	187.75	801	200.25	851	212.75	901	225.25	951	237.75
502	125.50	552	138.00	602	150.50	652	163.00	702	175.50	752	188.00	802	200.50	852	213.00	902	225.50	952	238.00
503	125.75	553	138.25	603	150.75	653	163.25	703	175.75	753	188.25	803	200.75	853	213.25	903	225.75	953	238.25
504	126.00	554	138.50	604	151.00	654	163.50	704	176.00	754	188.50	804	201.00	854	213.50	904	226.00	954	238.50
505	126.25	555	138.75	605	151.25	655	163.75	705	176.25	755	188.75	805	201.25	855	213.75	905	226.25	955	238.75
506	126.50	556	139.00	606	151.50	656	164.00	706	176.50	756	189.00	806	201.50	856	214.00	906	226.50	956	239.00
507	126.75	557	139.25	607	151.75	657	164.25	707	176.75	757	189.25	807	201.75	857	214.25	907	226.75	957	239.25
508	127.00	558	139.50	608	152.00	658	164.50	708	177.00	758	189.50	808	202.00	858	214.50	908	227.00	958	239.50
509	127.25	559	139.75	609	152.25	659	164.75	709	177.25	759	189.75	809	202.25	859	214.75	909	227.25	959	239.75
510	127.50	560	140.00	610	152.50	660	165.00	710	177.50	760	190.00	810	202.50	860	215.00	910	227.50	960	240.00
511	127.75	561	140.25	611	152.75	661	165.25	711	177.75	761	190.25	811	202.75	861	215.25	911	227.75	961	240.25
512	128.00	562	140.50	612	153.00	662	165.50	712	178.00	762	190.50	812	203.00	862	215.50	912	228.00	962	240.50
513	128.25	563	140.75	613	153.25	663	165.75	713	178.25	763	190.75	813	203.25	863	215.75	913	228.25	963	240.75
514	128.50	564	141.00	614	153.50	664	166.00	714	178.50	764	191.00	814	203.50	864	216.00	914	228.50	964	241.00
515	128.75	565	141.25	615	153.75	665	166.25	715	178.75	765	191.25	815	203.75	865	216.25	915	228.75	965	241.25
516	129.00	566	141.50	616	154.00	666	166.50	716	179.00	766	191.50	816	204.00	866	216.50	916	229.00	966	241.50
517	129.25	567	141.75	617	154.25	667	166.75	717	179.25	767	191.75	817	204.25	867	216.75	917	229.25	967	241.75
518	129.50	568	142.00	618	154.50	668	167.00	718	179.50	768	192.00	818	204.50	868	217.00	918	229.50	968	242.00
519	129.75	569	142.25	619	154.75	669	167.25	719	179.75	769	192.25	819	204.75	869	217.25	919	229.75	969	242.25
520	130.00	570	142.50	620	155.00	670	167.50	720	180.00	770	192.50	820	205.00	870	217.50	920	230.00	970	242.50
521	130.25	571	142.75	621	155.25	671	167.75	721	180.25	771	192.75	821	205.25	871	217.75	921	230.25	971	242.75
522	130.50	572	143.00	622	155.50	672	168.00	722	180.50	772	193.00	822	205.50	872	218.00	922	230.50	972	243.00
523	130.75	573	143.25	623	155.75	673	168.25	723	180.75	773	193.25	823	205.75	873	218.25	923	230.75	973	243.25
524	131.00	574	143.50	624	156.00	674	168.50	724	181.00	774	193.50	824	206.00	874	218.50	924	231.00	974	243.50
525	131.25	575	143.75	625	156.25	675	168.75	725	181.25	775	193.75	825	206.25	875	218.75	925	231.25	975	243.75
526	131.50	576	144.00	626	156.50	676	169.00	726	181.50	776	194.00	826	206.50	876	219.00	926	231.50	976	244.00
527	131.75	577	144.25	627	156.75	677	169.25	727	181.75	777	194.25	827	206.75	877	219.25	927	231.75	977	244.25
528	132.00	578	144.50	628	157.00	678	169.50	728	182.00	778	194.50	828	207.00	878	219.50	928	232.00	978	244.50
529	132.25	579	144.75	629	157.25	679	169.75	729	182.25	779	194.75	829	207.25	879	219.75	929	232.25	979	244.75
530	132.50	580	145.00	630	157.50	680	170.00	730	182.50	780	195.00	830	207.50	880	220.00	930	232.50	980	245.00
531	132.75	581	145.25	631	157.75	681	170.25	731	182.75	781	195.25	831	207.75	881	220.25	931	232.75	981	245.25
532	133.00	582	145.50	632	158.00	682	170.50	732	183.00	782	195.50	832	208.00	882	220.50	932	233.00	982	245.50
533	133.25	583	145.75	633	158.25	683	170.75	733	183.25	783	195.75	833	208.25	883	220.75	933	233.25	983	245.75
534	133.50	584	146.00	634	158.50	684	171.00	734	183.50	784	196.00	834	208.50	884	221.00	934	233.50	984	246.00
535	133.75	585	146.25	635	158.75	685	171.25	735	183.75	785	196.25	835	208.75	885	221.25	935	233.75	985	246.25
536	134.00	586	146.50	636	159.00	686	171.50	736	184.00	786	196.50	836	209.00	886	221.50	936	234.00	986	246.50
537	134.25	587	146.75	637	159.25	687	171.75	737	184.25	787	196.75	837	209.25	887	221.75	937	234.25	987	246.75
538	134.50	588	147.00	638	159.50	688	172.00	738	184.50	788	197.00	838	209.50	888	222.00	938	234.50	988	247.00
539	134.75	589	147.25	639	159.75	689	172.25	739	184.75	789	197.25	839	209.75	889	222.25	939	234.75	989	247.25
540	135.00	590	147.50	640	160.00	690	172.50	740	185.00	790	197.50	840	210.00	890	222.50	940	235.00	990	247.50
541	135.25	591	147.75	641	160.25	691	172.75	741	185.25	791	197.75	841	210.25	891	222.75	941	235.25	991	247.75
542	135.50	592	148.00	642	160.50	692	173.00	742	185.50	792	198.00	842	210.50	892	223.00	942	235.50	992	248.00
543	135.75	593	148.25	643	160.75	693	173.25	743	185.75	793	198.25	843	210.75	893	223.25	943	235.75	993	248.25
544	136.00	594	148.50	644	161.00	694	173.50	744	186.00	794	198.50	844	211.00	894	223.50	944	236.00	994	248.50
545	136.25	595	148.75	645	161.25	695	173.75	745	186.25	795	198.75	845	211.25	895	223.75	945	236.25	995	248.75
546	136.50	596	149.00	646	161.50	696	174.00	746	186.50	796	199.00	846	211.50	896	224.00	946	236.50	996	249.00
547	136.75	597	149.25	647	161.75	697	174.25	747	186.75	797	199.25	847	211.75	897	224.25	947	236.75	997	249.25
548	137.00	598	149.50	648	162.00	698	174.50	748	187.00	798	199.50	848	212.00	898	224.50	948	237.00	998	249.50
549	137.25	599	149.75	649	162.25	699	174.75	749	187.25	799	199.75	849	212.25	899	224.75	949	237.25	999	249.75
550	137.50	600	150.00	650	162.50	700	175.00	750	187.50	800	200.00	850	212.50	900	225.00	950	237.50	1,000	250.00
£5,500	£1,375	£6,000	£1,500	£6,500	£1,625	£7,000	£1,750	£7,500	£1,875	£8,000	£2,000	£8,500	£2,125	£9,000	£2,250	£9,500	£2,375	£10,000	£2,500

40% Income Tax Higher Rate 1994/95 (a)
Inheritance Tax: Rate from 15 March 1988 (b)

(a) Payable on taxable income over £23,700 (1993/94 £23,700)
(b) Payable on chargeable transfers over £150,000 after 9 March 1992

£ or p	Tax £ or p	£ or p	Tax £ or p	£	Tax £	£	Tax £	£	Tax £	£	Tax £	£	Tax £	£	Tax £	£	Tax £	£	Tax £
1	0·40	51	20·40	101	40·40	151	60·40	201	80·40	251	100·40	301	120·40	351	140·40	401	160·40	451	180·40
2	0·80	52	20·80	102	40·80	152	60·80	202	80·80	252	100·80	302	120·80	352	140·80	402	160·80	452	180·80
3	1·20	53	21·20	103	41·20	153	61·20	203	81·20	253	101·20	303	121·20	353	141·20	403	161·20	453	181·20
4	1·60	54	21·60	104	41·60	154	61·60	204	81·60	254	101·60	304	121·60	354	141·60	404	161·60	454	181·60
5	2·00	55	22·00	105	42·00	155	62·00	205	82·00	255	102·00	305	122·00	355	142·00	405	162·00	455	182·00
6	2·40	56	22·40	106	42·40	156	62·40	206	82·40	256	102·40	306	122·40	356	142·40	406	162·40	456	182·40
7	2·80	57	22·80	107	42·80	157	62·80	207	82·80	257	102·80	307	122·80	357	142·80	407	162·80	457	182·80
8	3·20	58	23·20	108	43·20	158	63·20	208	83·20	258	103·20	308	123·20	358	143·20	408	163·20	458	183·20
9	3·60	59	23·60	109	43·60	159	63·60	209	83·60	259	103·60	309	123·60	359	143·60	409	163·60	459	183·60
10	4·00	60	24·00	110	44·00	160	64·00	210	84·00	260	104·00	310	124·00	360	144·00	410	164·00	460	184·00
11	4·40	61	24·40	111	44·40	161	64·40	211	84·40	261	104·40	311	124·40	361	144·40	411	164·40	461	184·40
12	4·80	62	24·80	112	44·80	162	64·80	212	84·80	262	104·80	312	124·80	362	144·80	412	164·80	462	184·80
13	5·20	63	25·20	113	45·20	163	65·20	213	85·20	263	105·20	313	125·20	363	145·20	413	165·20	463	185·20
14	5·60	64	25·60	114	45·60	164	65·60	214	85·60	264	105·60	314	125·60	364	145·60	414	165·60	464	185·60
15	6·00	65	26·00	115	46·00	165	66·00	215	86·00	265	106·00	315	126·00	365	146·00	415	166·00	465	186·00
16	6·40	66	26·40	116	46·40	166	66·40	216	86·40	266	106·40	316	126·40	366	146·40	416	166·40	466	186·40
17	6·80	67	26·80	117	46·80	167	66·80	217	86·80	267	106·80	317	126·80	367	146·80	417	166·80	467	186·80
18	7·20	68	27·20	118	47·20	168	67·20	218	87·20	268	107·20	318	127·20	368	147·20	418	167·20	468	187·20
19	7·60	69	27·60	119	47·60	169	67·60	219	87·60	269	107·60	319	127·60	369	147·60	419	167·60	469	187·60
20	8·00	70	28·00	120	48·00	170	68·00	220	88·00	270	108·00	320	128·00	370	148·00	420	168·00	470	188·00
21	8·40	71	28·40	121	48·40	171	68·40	221	88·40	271	108·40	321	128·40	371	148·40	421	168·40	471	188·40
22	8·80	72	28·80	122	48·80	172	68·80	222	88·80	272	108·80	322	128·80	372	148·80	422	168·80	472	188·80
23	9·20	73	29·20	123	49·20	173	69·20	223	89·20	273	109·20	323	129·20	373	149·20	423	169·20	473	189·20
24	9·60	74	29·60	124	49·60	174	69·60	224	89·60	274	109·60	324	129·60	374	149·60	424	169·60	474	189·60
25	10·00	75	30·00	125	50·00	175	70·00	225	90·00	275	110·00	325	130·00	375	150·00	425	170·00	475	190·00
26	10·40	76	30·40	126	50·40	176	70·40	226	90·40	276	110·40	326	130·40	376	150·40	426	170·40	476	190·40
27	10·80	77	30·80	127	50·80	177	70·80	227	90·80	277	110·80	327	130·80	377	150·80	427	170·80	477	190·80
28	11·20	78	31·20	128	51·20	178	71·20	228	91·20	278	111·20	328	131·20	378	151·20	428	171·20	478	191·20
29	11·60	79	31·60	129	51·60	179	71·60	229	91·60	279	111·60	329	131·60	379	151·60	429	171·60	479	191·60
30	12·00	80	32·00	130	52·00	180	72·00	230	92·00	280	112·00	330	132·00	380	152·00	430	172·00	480	192·00
31	12·40	81	32·40	131	52·40	181	72·40	231	92·40	281	112·40	331	132·40	381	152·40	431	172·40	481	192·40
32	12·80	82	32·80	132	52·80	182	72·80	232	92·80	282	112·80	332	132·80	382	152·80	432	172·80	482	192·80
33	13·20	83	33·20	133	53·20	183	73·20	233	93·20	283	113·20	333	133·20	383	153·20	433	173·20	483	193·20
34	13·60	84	33·60	134	53·60	184	73·60	234	93·60	284	113·60	334	133·60	384	153·60	434	173·60	484	193·60
35	14·00	85	34·00	135	54·00	185	74·00	235	94·00	285	114·00	335	134·00	385	154·00	435	174·00	485	194·00
36	14·40	86	34·40	136	54·40	186	74·40	236	94·40	286	114·40	336	134·40	386	154·40	436	174·40	486	194·40
37	14·80	87	34·80	137	54·80	187	74·80	237	94·80	287	114·80	337	134·80	387	154·80	437	174·80	487	194·80
38	15·20	88	35·20	138	55·20	188	75·20	238	95·20	288	115·20	338	135·20	388	155·20	438	175·20	488	195·20
39	15·60	89	35·60	139	55·60	189	75·60	239	95·60	289	115·60	339	135·60	389	155·60	439	175·60	489	195·60
40	16·00	90	36·00	140	56·00	190	76·00	240	96·00	290	116·00	340	136·00	390	156·00	440	176·00	490	196·00
41	16·40	91	36·40	141	56·40	191	76·40	241	96·40	291	116·40	341	136·40	391	156·40	441	176·40	491	196·40
42	16·80	92	36·80	142	56·80	192	76·80	242	96·80	292	116·80	342	136·80	392	156·80	442	176·80	492	196·80
43	17·20	93	37·20	143	57·20	193	77·20	243	97·20	293	117·20	343	137·20	393	157·20	443	177·20	493	197·20
44	17·60	94	37·60	144	57·60	194	77·60	244	97·60	294	117·60	344	137·60	394	157·60	444	177·60	494	197·60
45	18·00	95	38·00	145	58·00	195	78·00	245	98·00	295	118·00	345	138·00	395	158·00	445	178·00	495	198·00
46	18·40	96	38·40	146	58·40	196	78·40	246	98·40	296	118·40	346	138·40	396	158·40	446	178·40	496	198·40
47	18·80	97	38·80	147	58·80	197	78·80	247	98·80	297	118·80	347	138·80	397	158·80	447	178·80	497	198·80
48	19·20	98	39·20	148	59·20	198	79·20	248	99·20	298	119·20	348	139·20	398	159·20	448	179·20	498	199·20
49	19·60	99	39·60	149	59·60	199	79·60	249	99·60	299	119·60	349	139·60	399	159·60	449	179·60	499	199·60
50	20·00	100	40·00	150	60·00	200	80·00	250	100·00	300	120·00	350	140·00	400	160·00	450	180·00	500	200·00

On Tax	£1,000 £400	£1,500 £600	£2,000 £800	£2,500 £1,000	£3,000 £1,200	£3,500 £1,400	£4,000 £1,600	£4,500 £1,800	£5,000 £2,000

(a) Payable on taxable income over £23,700 (1993/94 £23,700)
(b) Payable on chargeable transfers over £150,000 after 9 March 1992

Income Tax Higher Rate 1994/95 (a)   40%
Inheritance Tax: Rate from 15 March 1988 (b)

£	Tax £	£	Tax £	£	Tax £	£	Tax £	£	Tax £	£	Tax £	£	Tax £	£	Tax £	£	Tax £	£	Tax £
501	200·40	551	220·40	601	240·40	651	260·40	701	280·40	751	300·40	801	320·40	851	340·40	901	360·40	951	380·40
502	200·80	552	220·80	602	240·80	652	260·80	702	280·80	752	300·80	802	320·80	852	340·80	902	360·80	952	380·80
503	210·20	553	221·20	603	241·20	653	261·20	703	281·20	753	301·20	803	321·20	853	341·20	903	361·20	953	381·20
504	201·60	554	221·60	604	241·60	654	261·60	704	281·60	754	301·60	804	321·60	854	341·60	904	361·60	954	381·60
505	202·00	555	222·00	605	242·00	655	262·00	705	282·00	755	302·00	805	322·00	855	342·00	905	362·00	955	382·00
506	202·40	556	222·40	606	242·40	656	262·40	706	282·40	756	302·40	806	322·40	856	342·40	906	362·40	956	382·40
507	202·80	557	222·80	607	242·80	657	262·80	707	282·80	757	302·80	807	322·80	857	342·80	907	362·80	957	382·80
508	203·20	558	223·20	608	243·20	658	263·20	708	283·20	758	303·20	808	323·20	858	343·20	908	363·20	958	383·20
509	203·60	559	223·60	609	243·60	659	263·60	709	283·60	759	303·60	809	323·60	859	343·60	909	363·60	959	383·60
510	204·00	560	224·00	610	244·00	660	264·00	710	284·00	760	304·00	810	324·00	860	344·00	910	364·00	960	384·00
511	204·40	561	224·40	611	244·40	661	264·40	711	284·40	761	304·40	811	324·40	861	344·40	911	364·40	961	384·40
512	204·80	562	224·80	612	244·80	662	264·80	712	284·80	762	304·80	812	324·80	862	344·80	912	364·80	962	384·80
513	205·20	563	225·20	613	245·20	663	265·20	713	285·20	763	305·20	813	325·20	863	345·20	913	365·20	963	385·20
514	205·60	564	225·60	614	245·60	664	265·60	714	285·60	764	305·60	814	325·60	864	345·60	914	365·60	964	385·60
515	206·00	565	226·00	615	246·00	665	266·00	715	286·00	765	306·00	815	326·00	865	346·00	915	366·00	965	386·00
516	206·40	566	226·40	616	246·40	666	266·40	716	286·40	766	306·40	816	326·40	866	346·40	916	366·40	966	386·40
517	206·80	567	226·80	617	246·80	667	266·80	717	286·80	767	306·80	817	326·80	867	346·80	917	366·80	967	386·80
518	207·20	568	227·20	618	247·20	668	267·20	718	287·20	768	307·20	818	327·20	868	347·20	918	367·20	968	387·20
519	207·60	569	227·60	619	247·60	669	267·60	719	287·60	769	307·60	819	327·60	869	347·60	919	367·60	969	387·60
520	208·00	570	228·00	620	248·00	670	268·00	720	288·00	770	308·00	820	328·00	870	348·00	920	368·00	970	388·00
521	208·40	571	228·40	621	248·40	671	268·40	721	288·40	771	308·40	821	328·40	871	348·40	921	368·40	971	388·40
522	208·80	572	228·80	622	248·80	672	268·80	722	288·80	772	308·80	822	328·80	872	348·80	922	368·80	972	388·80
523	209·20	573	229·20	623	249·20	673	269·20	723	289·20	773	309·20	823	329·20	873	349·20	923	369·20	973	389·20
524	209·60	574	229·60	624	249·60	674	269·60	724	289·60	774	309·60	824	329·60	874	349·60	924	369·60	974	389·60
525	210·00	575	230·00	625	250·00	675	270·00	725	290·00	775	310·00	825	330·00	875	350·00	925	370·00	975	390·00
526	210·40	576	230·40	626	250·40	676	270·40	726	290·40	776	310·40	826	330·40	876	350·40	926	370·40	976	390·40
527	210·80	577	230·80	627	250·80	677	270·80	727	290·80	777	310·80	827	330·80	877	350·80	927	370·80	977	390·80
528	211·20	578	231·20	628	251·20	678	271·20	728	291·20	778	311·20	828	331·20	878	351·20	928	371·20	978	391·20
529	211·60	579	231·60	629	251·60	679	271·60	729	291·60	779	311·60	829	331·60	879	351·60	929	371·60	979	391·60
530	212·00	580	232·00	630	252·00	680	272·00	730	292·00	780	312·00	830	332·00	880	352·00	930	372·00	980	392·00
531	212·40	581	232·40	631	252·40	681	272·40	731	292·40	781	312·40	831	332·40	881	352·40	931	372·40	981	392·40
532	212·80	582	232·80	632	252·80	682	272·80	732	292·80	782	312·80	832	332·80	882	352·80	932	372·80	982	392·80
533	213·20	583	233·20	633	253·20	683	273·20	733	293·20	783	313·20	833	333·20	883	353·20	933	373·20	983	393·20
534	213·60	584	233·60	634	253·60	684	273·60	734	293·60	784	313·60	834	333·60	884	353·60	934	373·60	984	393·60
535	214·00	585	234·00	635	254·00	685	274·00	735	294·00	785	314·00	835	334·00	885	354·00	935	374·00	985	394·00
536	214·40	586	234·40	636	254·40	686	274·40	736	294·40	786	314·40	836	334·40	886	354·40	936	374·40	986	394·40
537	214·80	587	234·80	637	254·80	687	274·80	737	294·80	787	314·80	837	334·80	887	354·80	937	374·80	987	394·80
538	215·20	588	235·20	638	255·20	688	275·20	738	295·20	788	315·20	838	335·20	888	355·20	938	375·20	988	395·20
539	215·60	589	235·60	639	255·60	689	275·60	739	295·60	789	315·60	839	335·60	889	355·60	939	375·60	989	395·60
540	216·00	590	236·00	640	256·00	690	276·00	740	296·00	790	316·00	840	336·00	890	356·00	940	376·00	990	396·00
541	216·40	591	236·40	641	256·40	691	276·40	741	296·40	791	316·40	841	336·40	891	356·40	941	376·40	991	396·40
542	216·80	592	236·80	642	256·80	692	276·80	742	296·80	792	316·80	842	336·80	892	356·80	942	376·80	992	396·80
543	217·20	593	237·20	643	257·20	693	277·20	743	297·20	793	317·20	843	337·20	893	357·20	943	377·20	993	397·20
544	217·60	594	237·60	644	257·60	694	277·60	744	297·60	794	317·60	844	337·60	894	357·60	944	377·60	994	397·60
545	218·00	595	238·00	645	258·00	695	278·00	745	298·00	795	318·00	845	338·00	895	358·00	945	378·00	995	398·00
546	218·40	596	238·40	646	258·40	696	278·40	746	298·40	796	318·40	846	338·40	896	358·40	946	378·40	996	398·40
547	218·80	597	238·80	647	258·80	697	278·80	747	298·80	797	318·80	847	338·80	897	358·80	947	378·80	997	398·80
548	219·20	598	239·20	648	259·20	698	279·20	748	299·20	798	319·20	848	339·20	898	359·20	948	379·20	998	399·20
549	219·60	599	239·60	649	259·60	699	279·60	749	299·60	799	319·60	849	339·60	899	359·60	949	379·60	999	399·60
550	220·00	600	240·00	650	260·00	700	280·00	750	300·00	800	320·00	850	340·00	900	360·00	950	380·00	1,000	400·00
£5,500	**£2,200**	**£6,000**	**£2,400**	**£6,500**	**£2,600**	**£7,000**	**£2,800**	**£7,500**	**£3,000**	**£8,000**	**£3,200**	**£8,500**	**£3,400**	**£9,000**	**£3,600**	**£9,500**	**£3,800**	**£10,000**	**£4,000**

33% Corporation Tax: Full Rate F.Y. 1994

Rate of corporation tax payable on taxable profits of £1,500,000 and over for financial year 1994.

£ or p	Tax £ or p	£ or p	Tax £ or p	£	Tax £	£	Tax £	£	Tax £	£	Tax £	£	Tax £	£	Tax £	£	Tax £	£	Tax £
1	0·33	51	16·83	101	33·33	151	49·83	201	66·33	251	82·83	301	99·33	351	115·83	401	132·33	451	148·83
2	0·66	52	17·16	102	33·66	152	50·16	202	66·66	252	83·16	302	99·66	352	116·16	402	132·66	452	149·16
3	0·99	53	17·49	103	33·99	153	50·49	203	66·99	253	83·49	303	99·99	353	116·49	403	132·99	453	149·49
4	1·32	54	17·82	104	34·32	154	50·82	204	67·32	254	83·82	304	100·32	354	116·82	404	133·32	454	149·82
5	1·65	55	18·15	105	34·65	155	51·15	205	67·65	255	84·15	305	100·65	355	117·15	405	133·65	455	150·15
6	1·98	56	18·48	106	34·98	156	51·48	206	67·98	256	84·48	306	100·98	356	117·48	406	133·98	456	150·48
7	2·31	57	18·81	107	35·31	157	51·81	207	68·31	257	84·81	307	101·31	357	117·81	407	134·31	457	150·81
8	2·64	58	19·14	108	35·64	158	52·14	208	68·64	258	85·14	308	101·64	358	118·14	408	134·64	458	151·14
9	2·97	59	19·47	109	35·97	159	52·47	209	68·97	259	85·47	309	101·97	359	118·47	409	134·97	459	151·47
10	3·30	60	19·80	110	36·30	160	52·80	210	69·30	260	85·80	310	102·30	360	118·80	410	135·30	460	151·80
11	3·63	61	20·13	111	36·63	161	53·13	211	69·63	261	86·13	311	102·63	361	119·13	411	135·63	461	152·13
12	3·96	62	20·46	112	36·96	162	53·46	212	69·96	262	86·46	312	102·96	362	119·46	412	135·96	462	152·46
13	4·29	63	20·79	113	37·29	163	53·79	213	70·29	263	86·79	313	103·29	363	119·79	413	136·29	463	152·79
14	4·62	64	21·12	114	37·62	164	54·12	214	70·62	264	87·12	314	103·62	364	120·12	414	136·62	464	153·12
15	4·95	65	21·45	115	37·95	165	54·45	215	70·95	265	87·45	315	103·95	365	120·45	415	136·95	465	153·45
16	5·28	66	21·78	116	38·28	166	54·78	216	71·28	266	87·78	316	104·28	366	120·78	416	137·28	466	153·78
17	5·61	67	22·11	117	38·61	167	55·11	217	71·61	267	88·11	317	104·61	367	121·11	417	137·61	467	154·11
18	5·94	68	22·44	118	38·94	168	55·44	218	71·94	268	88·44	318	104·94	368	121·44	418	137·94	468	154·44
19	6·27	69	22·77	119	39·27	169	55·77	219	72·27	269	88·77	319	105·27	369	121·77	419	138·27	469	154·77
20	6·60	70	23·10	120	39·60	170	56·10	220	72·60	270	89·10	320	105·60	370	122·10	420	138·60	470	155·10
21	6·93	71	23·43	121	39·93	171	56·43	221	72·93	271	89·43	321	105·93	371	122·43	421	138·93	471	155·43
22	7·26	72	23·76	122	40·26	172	56·76	222	73·26	272	89·76	322	106·26	372	122·76	422	139·26	472	155·76
23	7·59	73	24·09	123	40·59	173	57·09	223	73·59	273	90·09	323	106·59	373	123·09	423	139·59	473	156·09
24	7·92	74	24·42	124	40·92	174	57·42	224	73·92	274	90·42	324	106·92	374	123·42	424	139·92	474	156·42
25	8·25	75	24·75	125	41·25	175	57·75	225	74·25	275	90·75	325	107·25	375	123·75	425	140·25	475	156·75
26	8·58	76	25·08	126	41·58	176	58·08	226	74·58	276	91·08	326	107·58	376	124·08	426	140·58	476	157·08
27	8·91	77	25·41	127	41·91	177	58·41	227	74·91	277	91·41	327	107·91	377	124·41	427	140·91	477	157·41
28	9·24	78	25·74	128	42·24	178	58·74	228	75·24	278	91·74	328	108·24	378	124·74	428	141·24	478	157·74
29	9·57	79	26·07	129	42·57	179	59·07	229	75·57	279	92·07	329	108·57	379	125·07	429	141·57	479	158·07
30	9·90	80	26·40	130	42·90	180	59·40	230	75·90	280	92·40	330	108·90	380	125·40	430	141·90	480	158·40
31	10·23	81	26·73	131	43·23	181	59·73	231	76·23	281	92·73	331	109·23	381	125·73	431	142·23	481	158·73
32	10·56	82	27·06	132	43·56	182	60·06	232	76·56	282	93·06	332	109·56	382	126·06	432	142·56	482	159·06
33	10·89	83	27·39	133	43·89	183	60·39	233	76·89	283	93·39	333	109·89	383	126·39	433	142·89	483	159·39
34	11·22	84	27·72	134	44·22	184	60·72	234	77·22	284	93·72	334	110·22	384	126·72	434	143·22	484	159·72
35	11·55	85	28·05	135	44·55	185	61·05	235	77·55	285	94·05	335	110·55	385	127·05	435	143·55	485	160·05
36	11·88	86	28·38	136	44·88	186	61·38	236	77·88	286	94·38	336	110·88	386	127·38	436	143·88	486	160·38
37	12·21	87	28·71	137	45·21	187	61·71	237	78·21	287	94·71	337	111·21	387	127·71	437	144·21	487	160·71
38	12·54	88	29·04	138	45·54	188	62·04	238	78·54	288	95·04	338	111·54	388	128·04	438	144·54	488	161·04
39	12·87	89	29·37	139	45·87	189	62·37	239	78·87	289	95·37	339	111·87	389	128·37	439	144·87	489	161·37
40	13·20	90	29·70	140	46·20	190	62·70	240	79·20	290	95·70	340	112·20	390	128·70	440	145·20	490	161·70
41	13·53	91	30·03	141	46·53	191	63·03	241	79·53	291	96·03	341	112·53	391	129·03	441	145·53	491	162·03
42	13·86	92	30·36	142	46·86	192	63·36	242	79·86	292	96·36	342	112·86	392	129·36	442	145·86	492	162·36
43	14·19	93	30·69	143	47·19	193	63·69	243	80·19	293	96·69	343	113·19	393	129·69	443	146·19	493	162·69
44	14·52	94	31·02	144	47·52	194	64·02	244	80·52	294	97·02	344	113·52	394	130·02	444	146·52	494	163·02
45	14·85	95	31·35	145	47·85	195	64·35	245	80·85	295	97·35	345	113·85	395	130·35	445	146·85	495	163·35
46	15·18	96	31·68	146	48·18	196	64·68	246	81·18	296	97·68	346	114·18	396	130·68	446	147·18	496	163·68
47	15·51	97	32·01	147	48·51	197	65·01	247	81·51	297	98·01	347	114·51	397	131·01	447	147·51	497	164·01
48	15·84	98	32·34	148	48·84	198	65·34	248	81·84	298	98·34	348	114·84	398	131·34	448	147·84	498	164·34
49	16·17	99	32·67	149	49·17	199	65·67	249	82·17	299	98·67	349	115·17	399	131·67	449	148·17	499	164·67
50	16·50	100	33·00	150	49·50	200	66·00	250	82·50	300	99·00	350	115·50	400	132·00	450	148·50	500	165·00

On	£1,000	£1,500	£2,000	£2,500	£3,000	£3,500	£4,000	£4,500	£5,000
Tax	£330	£495	£660	£825	£990	£1,155	£1,320	£1,485	£1,650

The Budget proposals as introduced by the Chancellor of the Exchequer in the House of Commons.
Note: It must be remembered that these proposals are subject to amendment during the passage of the Finance Bill.

Personal Taxation

	1993/94	1994/95
Personal allowance	£3,445	£3,445
Married couple's allowance	£1,720	£1,720
Addition re child if claimant single or claimant's wife ill	£1,720	£1,720
Widow's bereavement	£1,720	£1,720
Blind person	£1,080	**£1,200**
Age allowance income limit	£14,200	£14,200

Allowances where aged 65 to 74

Personal allowance	£4,200	£4,200
Married couple's allowance	£2,465	**£2,665**

Allowances where aged 75 or over

Personal allowance	£4,370	£4,370
Married couple's allowance	£2,505	**£2,705**

Income Tax Rates

Lower rate	20%	20%
on taxable income up to	£2,500	**£3,000**
Basic rate	25%	25%
on taxable income up to	£23,700	£23,700
Higher rate	40%	40%
on taxable income over	£23,700	£23,700

Capital Gains Tax

Rate	20%/25%/40%	20%/25%/40%
Exemption limit (per person)	£5,800	£5,800

Company Taxation

Corporation Tax Rates	FY 93	FY 94
All companies (except below)	33%	33%
Companies with small profits	25%	25%
– 25% rate relief	£250,000	**£300,000**
– marginal relief limit	£1,250,000	**£1,500,000**
– marginal Rates	35%	35%
Advance corporation tax rate	9/31	**1/4**

Inheritance Tax

For transfers after	9/3/92
Threshold	£150,000
Rate	40%

VAT

Standard rate	17.5%
Registration threshold	**£45,000**

after 30 November 1993 (previously £37,600)

National Insurance

1994/95 (1993/94 in brackets where different)

Class 1 Contributions

Employees

Below **£57 p.w.** (£56 p.w.)   NIL
from **£57 to £430** (£56 to £420) p.w., 2% up to **£57** (£56) p.w.
plus **10.0%** (9.0%) (contracted-out rate **8.2%** (7.2%)) up to **£430** (£420) p.w.

Employers

Weekly earnings	% contribution on all earnings*
0–£56.99 (0–£55.99)	NIL
£57.00 – £99.99 (£56.00–£94.99)	**3.60%** (4.60%)
£100.00 – £144.99 (£95.00–£139.99)	**5.60%** (6.60%)
£145.00 – £199.99 (£140.00–£194.99)	**7.60%** (8.60%)
Over **£199.99** (£194.99)	**10.20%** (10.40%)

* Contracted-out rates are 3.00% less on the excess earnings over **£57** (£56) p.w. up to **£430** (£420) p.w.

Class 1A contributions

Rate	**10.20%**	(10.40%)

Class 2 contributions

Flat weekly rate	**£5.65**	(£5.55)
Exemption limit	**£3,200**	(£3,140)

Class 3 contributions

Flat weekly rate	**£5.55**	(£5.45)

Class 4 contributions

Rate	**7.30%**	(6.30%)
Band	**£6,490 – £22,360**	(£6,340 – £21,840)

(Changes throughout shown in bold type)

Summary of Budget Proposals 30 November 1993

Income Tax

Income Tax Rates and Personal Allowances. For the tax year 1994/95, the first £3,000 (previously £2,500) of taxable income will be taxed at 20%. The basic rate limit remains at £23,700 (inclusive of the £3,000 lower rate band) and the basic and higher rates remain at 25% and 40% respectively.

The personal allowance remains unchanged, including the higher figures for older persons, as do the married couple's allowance for those aged under 65 and the other allowances linked to it. The married couple's allowances for those aged 65 and under 75, and for those aged 75 and over, are both increased by £200. The income limit for the age allowances remains at £14,200. The blind person's allowance is increased to £1,200.

Relief for the married couple's allowance (including the increased allowances for those aged 65 and over) and the other allowances linked to it, is restricted to 20% and is to be further restricted to 15% in 1995/96, when there will be a further increase of £330 in the age-related married couple's allowances.

Relief will be withdrawn for maintenance payments to or for certain children reaching the age of 21 after 5 April 1994.

Codes for 1994/95 taking account of these changes will be issued early in 1994.

Self-Assessment and Simplification of Personal Tax. It is proposed that the reforms announced in the March Budget will proceed, with some modifications.

Businesses commencing after 5 April 1994 will be assessed on the new current year basis. Existing businesses will move to the new basis with effect for 1997/98 and later years.

With effect for 1996/97 and later years, taxpayers who are required to complete a tax return will have the option to calculate their own liability to income tax and capital gains tax.

With effect from 31 January 1998, a uniform set of dates for the payment of income tax and capital gains tax is to be introduced.

MIRAS. Mortgage interest relief will continue to be limited to £30,000 but, from 6 April 1995, this relief will be restricted to 15% (20% from 6 April 1994).

Relief at the basic rate will continue to be available to people over 65 who take out certain loans for the purchase of life annuities.

Benefits in Kind. Loans provided by Employers. From 6 April 1994 there will be changes to the existing method of taxing cheap or interest-free loans to employees by employers.

In order to put employees with cheap or interest-free loans on the same footing as other mortgage borrowers who are to suffer the restriction in mortgage interest relief, there will be new rules to calculate the benefit. The interest on the loan will firstly be calculated at the 'official rate', then the employee will get tax relief within the ceiling of £30,000 on the mortgage interest actually paid and on the interest saved.

At present small loans are not taxed where the benefit does not exceed £300. This exemption is abolished and, instead, a new small loans exemption will apply where:
- all the employee's cheap or interest-free loans total no more than £5,000; or
- all the employee's loans, excluding loans qualifying for tax relief, do not exceed £5,000.

Loans made to employees on commercial terms by employers who lend to the general public will be exempt where:
- the loans are made by an employer whose business includes the lending of money;
- loans are made on the same conditions as to the general public;
- a substantial number of loans are made to public customers on those terms.

A new, lower, 'official rate' of interest will be set for certain foreign currency loans.

Finally, loans made in the normal course of domestic, family or personal relationships which are currently exempt will also apply to loans within families where the employer is a close company.

Company Cars. This Budget has no effect on the company car benefit rules mentioned in the last Budget which proposed a tax on 35% of the list price of the car from 6 April 1994.

The new car fuel scale charges to apply from 6 April 1994 are as follows:

Engine size	Scale charge 1993/94	Scale charge 1994/95
cc	£	£
Petrol		
0–1,400	600	640
1,401–2,000	760	810
2,001 +	1,130	1,200
Diesel		
0–2,000	550	580
2,001 +	710	750

The company car fuel scale charge is apportioned if the car is only available for part of a year. Also, the charge is only reduced to nil if the employee makes good *all* the fuel used for private journeys.

Note that car fuel scales are also used to calculate VAT on fuel provided by a business out of business resources for private motoring and to calculate Class 1A National Insurance Contributions.

Tax Relief for Vocational Training. From 1 January 1994 there will be tax relief for vocational training at level 5 of the National Vocational Qualifications and Scottish Vocational Qualifications. The intention is to broaden the tax relief so that it is available eventually at all levels. However, children under 16, and 16 to 18 year olds in full time education at school, will not benefit from the relief. Training for recreation or leisure activities will also be excluded from the relief.

Tax Relief for Private Medical Insurance. From 6 April 1994 it is proposed that tax relief on private medical insurance for the over 60s will be limited to 25%. Payers currently receive relief at their marginal rate or at 25% if non-taxpayers. Higher rate taxpayers will no longer be able to receive relief at their top rate. The relief will no longer enter into the calculation of income for any other tax purpose.

From 1 July 1994 it will no longer be necessary for insurers to obtain a certificate from the Inland Revenue before relief can be given.

Currently, for relief to be available to a married couple, only one spouse need be 60 or over, but if the older spouse dies, no relief is strictly due on any further premiums. For payments after 5 April 1994, the surviving spouse in such a case will receive relief for the remainder of the contract.

Under new rules from 1 July 1994, incentive payments costing less than £30 in connection with the taking out of medical insurance will not affect the relief.

The insurance premium tax which is to come into effect from October 1994 will be treated as part of the premium for tax relief purposes.

Benefits under Permanent Health Insurance Policies. A new extra-statutory concession has been issued to replace the existing concession. It will have effect when a policy holder first becomes entitled to certain insurance benefits on or after 6 April 1994. The benefits will be exempt from income tax for twelve months from the time the entitlement to benefit first arises, rather than for a period of between one and two years as at present. The concession will not apply to benefits payable to the employer, nor where the premiums are paid *by* the employer.

The existing concession continues to apply to accident and sickness policies where (a) a period of absence from work begins before and continues after 6 April 1994; (b) the absence is caused by sickness or disability; and (c) the policy holder has already become entitled to benefits before 6 April 1994 under one or more of these policies because of that absence from work.

Pensions

Improved Tax Regime for Personal Pensions. The operation of the tax regime for approved pension schemes will be improved. Personal pension scheme annuities paid after 6 April 1995 will be taxable on the same basis as pensions paid by occupational pension schemes. The monitoring of the tax affairs of occupational pension schemes, to make sure that the conditions on which tax reliefs are given continue to be met, will be improved. The requirement that the Inland Revenue approves the form of certain annuity contracts before they can be marketed to occupational pension schemes by insurance companies will be removed from 1 July 1994.

Pension Schemes Earnings Cap. The maximum level of earnings for which tax relief on pensions may be obtained will increase from £75,000 to £76,800 from 6 April 1994. The cap applies to all people who contribute to a personal pension scheme, who joined an occupational scheme set up since 14 March 1989 or who joined any occupational scheme since 1 June 1989.

Summary of Budget Proposals 30 November 1993

Capital Gains Tax

Annual Exempt Amount. The annual exempt amount for individuals for 1994/95 will remain at £5,800. The same exemption applies to personal representatives in the year of death and the two following years of assessment, and to trusts for mentally handicapped persons and those receiving certain disability allowances. The annual exempt amount for all other trusts will remain at £2,900.

Small Business Measures

Enterprise Investment Scheme. With effect from 1 January 1994 Enterprise Investment Scheme relief will be available for new equity investment in qualifying unquoted trading companies. The relief replaces the Business Expansion Scheme. The main features of the scheme are:
- relief at the lower rate of income tax (20%) on investments up to £100,000 per year;
- capital gains tax exemption on the first disposal of shares on which relief has not been withdrawn;
- relief against either income tax or capital gains tax for a loss on the first disposal of shares on which the original relief has not been withdrawn;
- a limit of £1 million on the amount a company can raise in a year on which relief will be given;
- an investor previously unconnected with the company or its trade is allowed to become a paid director while qualifying for relief.

The scheme will not extend to investment in private rented housing.

IHT: Replacement of Lifetime Gifts. Where someone receives a lifetime gift of business or agricultural property, the property can be sold, and, provided it is replaced within a year, business or agricultural relief will be available. The period for replacement is extended to three years for charges arising as a result of deaths on or after 30 November 1993.

Reinvestment Relief. A capital gains tax relief for entrepreneurs selling their own company and reinvesting in an unquoted trading company was introduced in the last Budget. Re-investment relief is now to be extended to make it available for all chargeable gains realised by individuals on disposals on or after Budget day. All chargeable gains of trustees will also be eligible for the new relief except where the beneficiaries of the trust are not individuals.

To qualify for relief the chargeable gain arising on any disposal must be re-invested in eligible shares in unquoted trading companies or in the holding company of a trading group. Re-investment must take place within a period beginning one year before and ending three years after the disposal. The main exclusions from the relief are re-investments in companies which hold more than half of their chargeable assets as land, farming companies, subsidiaries and certain financial concerns. The extended relief places no requirement on the investor to take a minimum holding in the unquoted company.

Retirement Relief. For disposals on or after Budget day, the limits applied in respect of capital gains tax retirement relief are raised so that full relief is available for the first £250,000 (previously £150,000) of gains and half relief is available on gains between £250,000 and £1,000,000 (previously between £150,000 and £600,000). The exemption is reduced if the individual has been running the business for less than 10 years.

Venture Capital Trusts. It is intended to issue a consultative document early in the New Year on a proposed new scheme of venture capital trusts. Legislation to enable this would be introduced in the 1995 Finance Bill. To qualify for the scheme the trust would have to invest a substantial proportion of its assets in unquoted trading companies. Dividends and capital gains relating to investors' holdings in the trust would be free of tax.

Debts given up in Voluntary Arrangements. The existing taxation rules are amended with effect from 30 November 1993 to make it easier for a creditor to obtain relief for trade debts given up as part of a voluntary arrangement under the 1986 Insolvency Act. As regards the debtor, the amount given up by the creditor will no longer be brought into charge to tax.

Inheritance Tax

The inheritance tax threshold will not be indexed and will remain at £150,000 for 1994/95.

Stamp Duty

Definition of 'Execution'. The definition of the 'execution' of a document has been clarified following suggestions from Scotland that this only required the signature of the document in question, rather than both signature and unconditional delivery, which has long been the Stamp Office's view. The new rule states that where a document is a deed which requires delivery in order to be effective, it will not be regarded as executed until it has been delivered. If delivered subject to conditions, it will not be executed until those conditions are fulfilled.

The new rule will apply to deeds executed on or after 8 December 1993 in all parts of the UK. For Scottish documents signed but not delivered before 8 December, the specific facts will determine whether the document has been executed.

Stamping of Agreements for Lease. Where the grant of a lease is preceded by an agreement for the lease, both instruments should strictly be stamped and credit for the duty paid on the agreement given against the duty payable on the grant. A new rule will relax the penalties for late stamping of an agreement by treating the agreement as made at the same time as the relevant lease and will apply to all agreements made on or after 6 May 1994. This will remove the need to present the agreement for stamping within 30 days of it being made to avoid a penalty.

Northern Ireland Documents. Regulations will be introduced to allow documents for transactions in Northern Ireland below the stamp duty threshold to be sent direct to the Registrar without first going to the Stamp Office. Similar arrangements already exist in the rest of the UK.

Corporation Tax

Rates and Profit Limits. The main and small companies' rates of corporation tax for financial year 1994 remain at 33% and 25% respectively, but the upper profit limit for the small companies' rate is increased to £300,000 (previously £250,000) and the marginal relief upper limit to £1,500,000 (previously £1,250,000).

The rate of advance corporation tax from 6 April 1994 is 1/4 (previously 9/31), as enacted in the 1993 Finance Act.

Anti-Avoidance Measures

The Chancellor has announced a package of measures designed to block loopholes and counter the avoidance of tax, as follows.
- From midnight on Budget day, it will no longer be possible to avoid National Insurance Contributions by paying employees in assets (for example, gold bars and coffee beans) which can then be converted into cash. Such payments will also be liable to tax under the PAYE system from some time in 1994.
- There are proposals to ensure that tax can continue to be collected under PAYE from certain employees who work partly in the UK and partly abroad.
- Changes are proposed to prevent the artificial exploitation of the profit-related pay rules for schemes registered after Budget day.
- For disposals on or after Budget day, capital gains tax indexation allowance is restricted. The allowance can only extinguish a capital gain. It can no longer be used to create or increase a capital loss.
- For expenditure incurred or contracted for on or after Budget day, a new rule will ensure that buildings and structures cannot qualify for capital allowances on machinery and plant. Also, a new time limit is introduced for notifying the Inland Revenue of expenditure on machinery and plant. The limit will normally be two years after the end of the year of assessment or company accounting period. If the time limit is missed, capital allowances can normally still be claimed but starting from a later year.
- Where a company is sold under a contract made on or after Budget day, new rules will make it easier for the Inland Revenue to collect from the former owners any unpaid corporation tax for accounting periods beginning before the sale.
- For accounting periods ending on or after Budget day, technical changes are made to prevent some of the profits of non-trading controlled foreign companies from escaping tax.
- Various measures attack certain devices aimed at avoiding or reducing stamp duty.
- A new rule will ensure that tax is charged on a benefit received from a

Summary of Budget Proposals 30 November 1993

funded unapproved retirement benefit scheme which has not itself been taxed in the UK.

- The rules on company residence will be changed so that certain dual resident companies will be regarded as non-UK resident for all tax purposes. Also, non-UK residents will get no tax relief for losses incurred as a result of royalty income being exempt from UK tax under a double tax treaty.
- The law on 'dividend manufacturing' is to be tightened.

Financial Sector Measures

Capital Gains Tax for Commodities and Derivatives. New rules will ensure that payments under commodity and financial futures contracts, and options which are settled in cash, are properly taken into account for capital gains purposes. This will apply to futures contracts entered into, and options granted, on or after 30 November 1993.

Tax for Authorised Unit Trusts. Authorised unit trusts will be liable to corporation tax in line with the basic rate of income tax. There are also to be new rules for trusts which invest in interest-bearing assets. These rules are to put investors receiving interest indirectly through an authorised unit trust in the same tax position as if they received that interest directly, thus removing a distortion in the domestic savings market. It will also have the effect of removing a tax barrier to the sale of authorised unit trusts to foreign investors. These changes will take effect for distribution periods beginning on or after 1 April 1994.

Taxation of Financial Instruments. The current complex system for taxing the profits and losses associated with financial instruments used by companies for managing interest rates and currency risks is to be simplified into one coherent regime broadly in line with the proposals in the Revenue's consultative document of August 1993. The date from which this will take effect has yet to be announced.

Review of Taxation of Interest. The rules for the taxation of interest paid and received by companies are to be reviewed.

The objectives of the review are to consider to what extent it is possible: that the system can be simplified by removing unnecessary distinctions between different ways of meeting the cost of borrowing and between loans from different types of lender; to allow the interest shown in the commercial accounts as a deduction for tax purposes; to remove the need to apportion the return on securities between capital and revenue; to rationalise the treatment of cross-border flows of interest to reflect international developments; and to make it easier for businesses to comply with their taxation responsibilities.

New Rules for Taxing FOREX. Proposals have been made to change further the legislation on the taxation of foreign exchange gains and losses. Regulations setting out detailed new rules will be published in draft form for further consultation. The legislation will not be brought into effect until at least three months after the regulations are finalised to allow

companies time to order their affairs taking the new rules into account.

New Procedures for MIRAS Lenders. The procedure by which lenders are admitted to the MIRAS scheme is to be streamlined. Although the criteria for qualification to become 'qualified lenders' will remain unchanged, the process will be faster and simpler from Royal Assent to the Finance Act.

Miscellaneous Business Measures

Late Payment Consultation. The Government are to issue a public consultation document on the late payment of commercial debt. The options to be considered to help solve this problem of particular concern to small business include legislation for a statutory right to interest and a British Standard on Prompt Payment.

Foreign Income Dividend Scheme. A UK company will be able to pay an optional foreign income dividend (FID) on or after 1 July 1994 out of a wide range of foreign-source profits in order to enable it to obtain a repayment of surplus advance corporation tax (ACT) in respect of that FID. This follows consultations announced in the previous Budget.

Tax Relief for Contributions to Business Links. A new tax relief for contributions by businesses (in cash or kind) to Business Links is to be introduced. Business Links is a new initiative to provide a single point of access for all key local business support agencies, including Training and Enterprise

Councils (TECs) and Local Enterprise Councils (LECs), which offer services to local businesses. The proposed relief will apply for payments made on or after 30 November 1993 and before 1 April 2000. It is proposed that the existing tax relief available for payments to TECs and LECs be extended to the same date.

Approved Profit-Sharing Schemes. There are to be two changes to the tax regime for approved profit-sharing schemes, whereby employees are allocated free shares in the company they work for. The shares initially have to be held in trust.

Where a male employee becomes chargeable to income tax in respect of shares allocated to him under a scheme approved before 25 July 1991, he will not be chargeable on a greater amount than a woman of similar age. This change is effective for tax charges resulting from events occurring on or after 30 November 1993.

In addition, Qualifying Corporate Bonds (QCBs) received by trustees on a reorganisation or take-over on or after the date of Royal Assent to the Finance Act, may be retained in trust and in due course distributed tax-free to scheme members.

Capital Allowances: Sales of Assets between Connected Persons. The provisions introduced in the Finance Act 1993 to allow connected persons to elect to transfer commercial buildings in enterprise zones and qualifying hotels on or after 16 March 1993 at their tax written-down values are to be extended to transfers taking place before that date.

National Insurance Contributions

Class 1 Contributions. From 6 April 1994, the lower earnings limit is raised to £57 per week and the upper earnings limit to £430 per week. The bands are also increased as shown on page 1. The main rate payable by employees on earnings between these limits is increased to 10% from 9%. The standard rate of employers' contributions is reduced to 10.2% from 10.4%. The reduced employers' rates for lower-paid workers are decreased by 1%.

Class 2 and Class 3 Contributions. From 6 April 1994, these are each increased by 10p to £5.65 and £5.55 per week respectively.

Class 4 Contributions. From 6 April 1994, the rate is increased to 7.3% from 6.3%. The annual limits of profits are raised to £6,490 and £22,360.

Loophole closed. With effect from Budget day, measures are introduced which ensure that any payments to employees in gold, other tradeable assets (principally commodities) or vouchers in respect of them will be subject to National Insurance Contributions.

Social Security Benefits

Help for VAT on Fuel. All pensioners, widows, the long-term sick on invalidity benefit and those on low incomes will receive extra help to meet the cost of VAT on their fuel bills.

The relief will take two forms, depending on the individual concerned.

From April 1994, pensioners on a full basic pension, widows and war widows, people receiving invalidity benefit, invalid care allowance, severe disablement allowance and war pensions unemployability supplement, and disabled people on income support will receive 50p per week for a single person on top of the normal benefit uprating (or 70p if there is a dependent spouse). If both members of a couple are receiving one of these benefits or a full pension, they will each receive 50p. From April 1995, when the VAT rate rises to 17.5%, the additional payments will rise to £1 or £1.40 as appropriate.

For households on income support (other than pensioners and disabled people), individuals will receive help by way of a further uprating in benefit from April 1994 of 0.4%. Persons receiving other income-related benefits such as family credit and housing benefit will see similar increases in benefit entitlement. A similar approach will operate in April 1995 when the VAT rises.

The social fund cold weather payments will increase from £6 to £7 per week next winter and to £7.50 the following winter. Also, all pensioners and disabled people will qualify for energy efficiency grants.

Annual Uprating. All major benefits will be uprated at least in line with the increase in the Retail Prices Index to September, which this year is 1.8%. The increase will take effect in the first full week of the 1994/95 tax year, i.e. the week beginning 11 April 1994.

Summary of Budget Proposals 30 November 1993

Value Added Tax

Registration and Deregistration Limits.
The annual registration limit for VAT is increased to £45,000 from £37,600 and the limit for those considering cancelling their registration is increased to £43,000 from £36,000. Both changes have effect from midnight on 30 November.

With effect from 1 January 1994, the registration and deregistration limits for acquisitions from other EC countries are both raised to £45,000 from £37,600.

Car Fuel Scales.
The scale charges for VAT on fuel used for private mileage in business cars are to be increased in line with the income tax charges.

The revised figures are as follows.

Quarterly returns

Cylinder capacity of vehicle	Scale charge diesel £	VAT due per car £	Scale charge petrol £	VAT due per car £
1,400cc or less	145	21.60	160	23.83
More than 1,400cc but not more than 2,000cc	145	21.60	202	30.09
More than 2,000cc	187	27.85	300	44.68

Monthly returns

Cylinder capacity of vehicle	Scale charge diesel £	VAT due per car £	Scale charge petrol £	VAT due per car £
1,400cc or less	48	7.15	53	7.89
More than 1,400cc but not more than 2,000cc	48	7.15	67	9.98
More than 2,000cc	62	9.23	100	14.89

Repayment Supplement.
Three changes are proposed: the time allowed for Customs and Excise to investigate a repayment claim before a supplement becomes payable is to be reduced; the minimum supplement payable is to be increased to £50 from £30; late repayment claims will no longer be eligible for supplement.

Insolvent Traders.
It is proposed that insolvent businesses should be allowed VAT credits even where there is also a VAT debt. At present, VAT repayments due to businesses in bankruptcy, liquidation or trading under a Voluntary Arrangement are, by concession, not set off against liabilities arising before the date of insolvency. The proposal puts the concession on a statutory basis and extends this treatment to businesses trading in Administrative Receivership or under Administration Orders. The new measures are to take effect shortly after Royal Assent to the 1994 Finance Act.

Car Leasing.
With effect from 1 January 1994, businesses which lease cars to taxi firms, self-drive hire firms and driving schools will be able to recover input tax paid on cars purchased for that purpose. Output tax on the eventual sale of the car will also have to be accounted for.

Tax on Expenditure

Betting and Gaming.
A package of measures to restructure and simplify the administrative arrangements for the issue of gaming licences is to be introduced. The move is part of the Government's deregulation initiative and follows consultation with trade bodies.

The intention is to reduce bureaucracy for the industry and to improve the collection and administration of the duty by allowing gaming machine operators to choose the licence periods which suit their operational needs rather than tying them to quarterly, half-yearly or annual licence periods. The measures will come into effect on 1 May 1994 for most traders and on 1 March 1994 for those who only operate over the summer season (i.e. April to September).

Vehicles, Alcohol and Tobacco.
The duty (including VAT) on leaded and unleaded petrol and on diesel is

increased by 3p a litre (14p a gallon), effective from 6pm on 30 November 1993. The Government's commitment to raising road fuel duties in real terms will continue in future Budgets, with the average planned increase rising from 3% to 5%.

Vehicle excise duty on cars, light goods vehicles, taxis and trade licences will increase to £130 from £125. The duty on lorries will remain largely unchanged. A new class of vehicle excise duty will be introduced for certain articulated lorries.

The duty on table and sparkling wines and on cider will increase broadly in line with inflation, but the increases are deferred until 1 January 1994. There is no increase in the duty on beer or spirits.

The duty on all tobacco products is increased by 7.3%, effective from 6pm on 30 November 1993. In future duty on tobacco will increase in real terms by at least 3% per year on average.

Air Passenger Duty. Excise duty is to be raised on air travel from UK airports from 1 October 1994. Passengers will be charged £5 for flights to UK and other EC destinations, and £10 elsewhere. This will be collected from passengers and paid to Customs and Excise by airlines. Exempt from the duty will be children under two who travel free, passengers on the return leg of a journey within the UK on a return ticket, transit and transfer passengers and passengers on small aircraft such as those used for Scottish inter-island services.

Customs Measures

Changes to Excise Law. A number of changes are proposed to existing excise law. These are as follows:

Assessment of Duty Due. Existing powers to estimate duty due from excise traders will be repealed. Excise officers will in future be required to exercise their best judgement in making assessments. Assessments will be required to be made within one year of the facts becoming known to Customs and Excise and normally within six years of the events giving rise to the assessment. Exceptions arise in the case of fraud.

Assessments will be appealable to the new VAT and Duties Tribunals (see below).

Decriminalisation of Breaches of Regulations. Currently breaches of excise regulations may be punished in the criminal courts with fines up to £5,000. Many minor breaches will be decriminalised and a system of fixed penalties introduced. The new civil penalties will be set at £250 for all offences, except:
- failure to pay duty due where the penalty will be £250 or 5% of the duty (whichever is greater); and
- £20 for each day on which there is a continuing failure (such as failure to maintain accounts and records).

Fraudulent Evasion of Excise Duties. HM Customs and Excise will have an option to treat fraudulent evasion of excise duties as either a civil or criminal matter. When a civil evasion penalty is imposed it will be payable on top of the arrears due and will be equal to those arrears. Powers will exist to reduce or cancel the penalty if there are mitigating circumstances. Any penalty imposed under these new powers will be appealable to the VAT and Duties Tribunals.

Independent Appeals Tribunals. With effect from 1 January 1995 a new two-stage system will be introduced to resolve most disputes involving Customs and Excise matters. The first stage will involve a Departmental review. If this fails to resolve the dispute the new system will allow for an appeal to independent VAT and Duties Tribunals. The jurisdiction of existing VAT Tribunals will be extended to cover these areas.

Reform of Customs Powers. With effect from the date of Royal Assent to the Finance Act new powers will be available to Customs officers for access to information from businesses involved in the importation and exportation of goods. These proposals will allow the Department to make regulations requiring businesses involved in a customs activity to keep records, and to produce them for inspection within such time and in such form as may reasonably be required. Such records may be copied or removed by officers.

It is the intention that these new provisions should align Customs' powers with those already in force for VAT and Excise.

Miscellaneous

Information on Non-Resident Trusts. The circumstances in which information must be provided about certain transactions involving non-resident trusts have been clarified, to ensure that the existing obligations to provide the Inland Revenue with information about, for example, the setting up of new trusts off-shore and of resident trusts emigrating, apply in all cases.

Jobseeker's Allowance. Steps to get unemployed people back to work as soon as possible will come into effect in 1996. The Jobseeker's Allowance will be a simpler, clearer system than that presently in operation.

Under the new system, people who qualify for benefit because of their National Insurance Contributions will be eligible for a personal allowance for six months. Those who are still unemployed after six months will be eligible for the allowance on a means-tested basis for as long as they need it, provided that they are genuinely looking for work.

National Savings: Pensioners Guaranteed Income Bond. A new bond, the National Savings Pensioners Guaranteed Income Bond, is to be introduced in 1994. The bond will be available only to savers aged 65 and over. Interest will be paid gross and at a rate which is guaranteed for five years.

Insurance Premium Tax. A new tax will apply to most general insurance premiums where the insured risk is located in the UK. With effect from 1 October 1994, Insurance Premium Tax (IPT) will be payable by the policyholder at the rate of 3%. The responsibility for collection and accounting to Customs and Excise for the tax will rest with the insurer. IPT will not apply to long-term insurance such as life insurance or pensions.

Inheritance Tax

LIFETIME TRANSFERS after 17 March 1986

(A) **Gifts to individuals, and gifts into accumulation and maintenance trusts, trusts for the disabled and, after 16 March 1987, transfers to and from certain interest in possession trusts:**

(i) *On or within seven years of death:*

On death, the full Death rates opposite apply, with a tapered reduction in the tax payable on transfers as follows:

Years between gift & death	Percentage of full charge at death rates
Not more than 3	100
More than 3 but not more than 4	80
More than 4 but not more than 5	60
More than 5 but not more than 6	40
More than 6 but not more than 7	20

Notes: (a) The scale in force at date of death applies
(b) Where a gift made before 18 March 1986 is chargeable as a result of the donor's death on or after 18 March 1986, no more tax will be payable under the IHT regime than if the previous CTT regime had continued

(ii) *More than seven years before death:*
NIL tax payable

(B) **Gifts involving transfers to and from and charges involving discretionary and certain other trusts, and gifts involving companies:**

At time of gift, **half** the Death rates opposite apply. If the gift also falls within seven years of death, (A)(i) above applies but the lifetime tax will be credited against tax due on death.

TRANSFERS ON DEATH (or within three years of death)

After 5 April 1989 and before 6 April 1990

	Chargeable transfer	Rate
(On)	£	%
First	118,000	Nil
Over	118,000	40

After 5 April 1990 and before 6 April 1991

	Chargeable transfer	Rate
(On)	£	%
First	128,000	Nil
Over	128,000	40

After 5 April 1991 and before 10 March 1992

	Chargeable transfer	Rate
(On)	£	%
First	140,000	Nil
Over	140,000	40

After 9 March 1992

	Chargeable transfer	Rate
(On)	£	%
First	150,000	Nil
Over	150,000	40

Main Taxable National Insurance Benefits
(All assessable under Schedule E)

	From 12.4.93 £	Taxable 1993-94 £	From 11.4.94 £	Taxable 1994-95 £
Retirement Pension (a)				
Married couple – both contributors: **each**	56.10	2,917	57.60	2,995
– wife non-contributor: joint	89.80	4,670	92.10	4,789
Single person	56.10	2,917	57.60	2,995
Old Person's Pension				
Married couple (both over 80)	67.90	3,531	69.50	3,614
Single person or married man (wife under 80)	33.95	1,765	34.75	1,807
Married woman (husband under 80)	33.95	1,765	34.75	1,807
Widow's Benefit				
Widowed Mother's Allowance (b)	56.10	2,917	57.60	2,995
Widow's Pension (b)	56.10	2,917	57.60	2,995
Industrial Death Benefit				
Widow's Pension				
Higher permanent rate	56.10	2,917	57.60	2,995
Lower permanent rate	16.83	875	17.28	899
Invalidity Allowance (c)				
Age when incapacity began:				
Under 40	11.95	621	12.15	632
40 to 49	7.50	390	7.60	395
50 to 60 (men), 55 (women)	3.75	195	3.80	198
Invalid Care Allowance				
Single	33.70	1,752	34.50	1,794
Increase for wife	20.15	1,048	20.65	1,074
Unemployment Benefit				
Single	44.65	2,322	45.45	2,363
Increase for dependent adult	27.55	1,433	28.05	1,459

(a) If pensioner is aged 80 or over, an additional 25p is payable.
(b) Standard rate of basic benefit, excluding any earnings-related 'additional pension'.
(c) Taxable only when paid with retirement pension.

Rate of corporation tax payable on taxable profits from £300,000 to £1,500,000 for financial year 1994.

Corporation Tax: Marginal Rate F.Y. 1994   35%

£ or p	Tax £ or p	£ or p	Tax £ or p	£	Tax £	£	Tax £	£	Tax £	£	Tax £	£	Tax £	£	Tax £	£	Tax £	£	Tax £
1	0·35	51	17·85	101	35·35	151	52·85	201	70·35	251	87·85	301	105·35	351	122·85	401	140·35	451	157·85
2	0·70	52	18·20	102	35·70	152	53·20	202	70·70	252	88·20	302	105·70	352	123·20	402	140·70	452	158·20
3	1·05	53	18·55	103	36·05	153	53·55	203	71·05	253	88·55	303	106·05	353	123·55	403	141·05	453	158·55
4	1·40	54	18·90	104	36·40	154	53·90	204	71·40	254	88·90	304	106·40	354	123·90	404	141·40	454	158·90
5	1·75	55	19·25	105	36·75	155	54·25	205	71·75	255	89·25	305	106·75	355	124·25	405	141·75	455	159·25
6	2·10	56	19·60	106	37·10	156	54·60	206	72·10	256	89·60	306	107·10	356	124·60	406	142·10	456	159·60
7	2·45	57	19·95	107	37·45	157	54·95	207	72·45	257	89·95	307	107·45	357	124·95	407	142·45	457	159·95
8	2·80	58	20·30	108	37·80	158	55·30	208	72·80	258	90·30	308	107·80	358	125·30	408	142·80	458	160·30
9	3·15	59	20·65	109	38·15	159	55·65	209	73·15	259	90·65	309	108·15	359	125·65	409	143·15	459	160·65
10	3·50	60	21·00	110	38·50	160	56·00	210	73·50	260	91·00	310	108·50	360	126·00	410	143·50	460	161·00
11	3·85	61	21·35	111	38·85	161	56·35	211	73·85	261	91·35	311	108·85	361	126·35	411	143·85	461	161·35
12	4·20	62	21·70	112	39·20	162	56·70	212	74·20	262	91·70	312	109·20	362	126·70	412	144·20	462	161·70
13	4·55	63	22·05	113	39·55	163	57·05	213	74·55	263	92·05	313	109·55	363	127·05	413	144·55	463	162·05
14	4·90	64	22·40	114	39·90	164	57·40	214	74·90	264	92·40	314	109·90	364	127·40	414	144·90	464	162·40
15	5·25	65	22·75	115	40·25	165	57·75	215	75·25	265	92·75	315	110·25	365	127·75	415	145·25	465	162·75
16	5·60	66	23·10	116	40·60	166	58·10	216	75·60	266	93·10	316	110·60	366	128·10	416	145·60	466	163·10
17	5·95	67	23·45	117	40·95	167	58·45	217	75·95	267	93·45	317	110·95	367	128·45	417	145·95	467	163·45
18	6·30	68	23·80	118	41·30	168	58·80	218	76·30	268	93·80	318	111·30	368	128·80	418	146·30	468	163·80
19	6·65	69	24·15	119	41·65	169	59·15	219	76·65	269	94·15	319	111·65	369	129·15	419	146·65	469	164·15
20	7·00	70	24·50	120	42·00	170	59·50	220	77·00	270	94·50	320	112·00	370	129·50	420	147·00	470	164·50
21	7·35	71	24·85	121	42·35	171	59·85	221	77·35	271	94·85	321	112·35	371	129·85	421	147·35	471	164·85
22	7·70	72	25·20	122	42·70	172	60·20	222	77·70	272	95·20	322	112·70	372	130·20	422	147·70	472	165·20
23	8·05	73	25·55	123	43·05	173	60·55	223	78·05	273	95·55	323	113·05	373	130·55	423	148·05	473	165·55
24	8·40	74	25·90	124	43·40	174	60·90	224	78·40	274	95·90	324	113·40	374	130·90	424	148·40	474	165·90
25	8·75	75	26·25	125	43·75	175	61·25	225	78·75	275	96·25	325	113·75	375	131·25	425	148·75	475	166·25
26	9·10	76	26·60	126	44·10	176	61·60	226	79·10	276	96·60	326	114·10	376	131·60	426	149·10	476	166·60
27	9·45	77	26·95	127	44·45	177	61·95	227	79·45	277	96·95	327	114·45	377	131·95	427	149·45	477	166·95
28	9·80	78	27·30	128	44·80	178	62·30	228	79·80	278	97·30	328	114·80	378	132·30	428	149·80	478	167·30
29	10·15	79	27·65	129	45·15	179	62·65	229	80·15	279	97·65	329	115·15	379	132·65	429	150·15	479	167·65
30	10·50	80	28·00	130	45·50	180	63·00	230	80·50	280	98·00	330	115·50	380	133·00	430	150·50	480	168·00
31	10·85	81	28·35	131	45·85	181	63·35	231	80·85	281	98·35	331	115·85	381	133·35	431	150·85	481	168·35
32	11·20	82	28·70	132	46·20	182	63·70	232	81·20	282	98·70	332	116·20	382	133·70	432	151·20	482	168·70
33	11·55	83	29·05	133	46·55	183	64·05	233	81·55	283	99·05	333	116·55	383	134·05	433	151·55	483	169·05
34	11·90	84	29·40	134	46·90	184	64·40	234	81·90	284	99·40	334	116·90	384	134·40	434	151·90	484	169·40
35	12·25	85	29·75	135	47·25	185	64·75	235	82·25	285	99·75	335	117·25	385	134·75	435	152·25	485	169·75
36	12·60	86	30·10	136	47·60	186	65·10	236	82·60	286	100·10	336	117·60	386	135·10	436	152·60	486	170·10
37	12·95	87	30·45	137	47·95	187	65·45	237	82·95	287	100·45	337	117·95	387	135·45	437	152·95	487	170·45
38	13·30	88	30·80	138	48·30	188	65·80	238	83·30	288	100·80	338	118·30	388	135·80	438	153·30	488	170·80
39	13·65	89	31·15	139	48·65	189	66·15	239	83·65	289	101·15	339	118·65	389	136·15	439	153·65	489	171·15
40	14·00	90	31·50	140	49·00	190	66·50	240	84·00	290	101·50	340	119·00	390	136·50	440	154·00	490	171·50
41	14·35	91	31·85	141	49·35	191	66·85	241	84·35	291	101·85	341	119·35	391	136·85	441	154·35	491	171·85
42	14·70	92	32·20	142	49·70	192	67·20	242	84·70	292	102·20	342	119·70	392	137·20	442	154·70	492	172·20
43	15·05	93	32·55	143	50·05	193	67·55	243	85·05	293	102·55	343	120·05	393	137·55	443	155·05	493	172·55
44	15·40	94	32·90	144	50·40	194	67·90	244	85·40	294	102·90	344	120·40	394	137·90	444	155·40	494	172·90
45	15·75	95	33·25	145	50·75	195	68·25	245	85·75	295	103·25	345	120·75	395	138·25	445	155·75	495	173·25
46	16·10	96	33·60	146	51·10	196	68·60	246	86·10	296	103·60	346	121·10	396	138·60	446	156·10	496	173·60
47	16·45	97	33·95	147	51·45	197	68·95	247	86·45	297	103·95	347	121·45	397	138·95	447	156·45	497	173·95
48	16·80	98	34·30	148	51·80	198	69·30	248	86·80	298	104·30	348	121·80	398	139·30	448	156·80	498	174·30
49	17·15	99	34·65	149	52·15	199	69·65	249	87·15	299	104·65	349	122·15	399	139·65	449	157·15	499	174·65
50	17·50	100	35·00	150	52·50	200	70·00	250	87·50	300	105·00	350	122·50	400	140·00	450	157·50	500	175·00
On Tax		£1,000 £350		£1,500 £525		£2,000 £700		£2,500 £875		£3,000 £1,050		£3,500 £1,225		£4,000 £1,400		£4,500 £1,575		£5,000 £1,750	

Take Home Pay: From 6 April 1994: (A) Not Contracted Out

* Or married woman not liable at redu... rate of national insura...
** Liable at reduced rate of national insura...

GROSS PAY Per Annum Up to £	GROSS PAY Per Month £	GROSS PAY Per Week £	NET TAKE HOME PAY per week Single Person * £	NET TAKE HOME PAY per week Married Man £	NET TAKE HOME PAY per week Married Woman or Widow ** £	COST TO EMPLOYER per week £
2,963.48	246.96	56.99	56.99	56.99	56.99	56.99
2,964.00	247.00	57.00	55.86	55.86	54.81	59.05
3,016.00	251.33	58.00	56.76	56.76	55.77	60.09
3,068.00	255.67	59.00	57.66	57.66	56.73	61.12
3,120.00	260.00	60.00	58.56	58.56	57.69	62.16
3,172.00	264.33	61.00	59.46	59.46	58.65	63.20
3,224.00	268.67	62.00	60.36	60.36	59.61	64.23
3,276.00	273.00	63.00	61.26	61.26	60.57	65.27
3,328.00	277.33	64.00	62.16	62.16	61.54	66.30
3,380.00	281.67	65.00	63.06	63.06	62.50	67.34
3,432.00	286.00	66.00	63.96	63.96	63.46	68.38
3,445.00	287.08	66.25	64.19	64.19	63.70	68.64
3,484.00	290.33	67.00	64.71	64.86	64.27	69.41
For each additional			Add			
52.00	4.33	1.00	0.70	0.90	0.76	1.04
104.00	8.67	2.00	1.40	1.80	1.52	2.07
156.00	13.00	3.00	2.10	2.70	2.28	3.11
208.00	17.33	4.00	2.80	3.60	3.05	4.14
260.00	21.67	5.00	3.50	4.50	3.81	5.18
312.00	26.00	6.00	4.20	5.40	4.57	6.22
364.00	30.33	7.00	4.90	6.30	5.33	7.25
416.00	34.67	8.00	5.60	7.20	6.09	8.29
468.00	39.00	9.00	6.30	8.10	6.85	9.32
520.00	43.33	10.00	7.00	9.00	7.62	10.36
5,148.00	429.00	99.00	87.11	93.66	88.64	102.56
5,165.16	430.43	99.33	87.34	93.96	88.89	102.91
5,199.48	433.29	99.99	87.80	94.42	89.39	103.59
5,200.00	433.33	100.00	87.81	94.43	89.40	105.60
5,252.00	437.67	101.00	88.51	95.13	90.16	106.66
5,304.00	442.00	102.00	89.21	95.83	90.92	107.71
5,356.00	446.33	103.00	89.91	96.53	91.68	108.77
5,408.00	450.67	104.00	90.61	97.23	92.45	109.82
5,460.00	455.00	105.00	91.31	97.93	93.21	110.88
5,512.00	459.33	106.00	92.01	98.63	93.97	111.94
5,564.00	463.67	107.00	92.71	99.33	94.73	112.99
5,616.00	468.00	108.00	93.41	100.03	95.49	114.05
5,668.00	472.33	109.00	94.11	100.73	96.25	115.10
5,720.00	476.67	110.00	94.81	101.43	97.02	116.16
5,772.00	481.00	111.00	95.51	102.13	97.78	117.22
5,824.00	485.33	112.00	96.21	102.83	98.54	118.27
5,876.00	489.67	113.00	96.91	103.53	99.30	119.33
5,928.00	494.00	114.00	97.61	104.23	100.06	120.38
5,980.00	498.33	115.00	98.31	104.93	100.82	121.44
6,032.00	502.67	116.00	99.01	105.63	101.58	122.50
6,084.00	507.00	117.00	99.71	106.33	102.35	123.55
6,136.00	511.33	118.00	100.41	107.03	103.11	124.61
6,188.00	515.67	119.00	101.11	107.73	103.87	125.66
6,240.00	520.00	120.00	101.81	108.43	104.63	126.72
6,292.00	524.33	121.00	102.51	109.13	105.39	127.78
6,344.00	528.67	122.00	103.21	109.83	106.15	128.83
6,396.00	533.00	123.00	103.91	110.53	106.91	129.89
6,444.88	537.07	123.94	104.57	111.18	107.63	130.88
6,448.00	537.33	124.00	104.61	111.23	107.67	130.94

GROSS PAY Per Annum Up to £	GROSS PAY Per Month £	GROSS PAY Per Week £	NET TAKE HOME PAY per week Single Person * £	NET TAKE HOME PAY per week Married Man £	NET TAKE HOME PAY per week Married Woman or Widow ** £	COST TO EMPLOYER per week £
For each additional			Add			
52.00	4.33	1.00	0.65	0.70	0.71	1.06
104.00	8.67	2.00	1.30	1.40	1.42	2.11
156.00	13.00	3.00	1.95	2.10	2.13	3.17
208.00	17.33	4.00	2.60	2.80	2.85	4.22
260.00	21.67	5.00	3.25	3.50	3.56	5.28
312.00	26.00	6.00	3.90	4.20	4.27	6.34
364.00	30.33	7.00	4.55	4.90	4.98	7.39
416.00	34.67	8.00	5.20	5.60	5.69	8.45
468.00	39.00	9.00	5.85	6.30	6.40	9.50
520.00	43.33	10.00	6.50	7.00	7.12	10.56
7,539.48	628.29	144.99	118.25	125.92	122.61	153.11
7,540.00	628.33	145.00	118.26	125.93	122.61	156.02
7,592.00	632.67	146.00	118.91	126.63	123.33	157.10
7,644.00	637.00	147.00	119.56	127.33	124.04	158.17
7,696.00	641.33	148.00	120.21	128.03	124.75	159.25
7,748.00	645.67	149.00	120.86	128.73	125.46	160.32
7,800.00	650.00	150.00	121.51	129.43	126.17	161.40
7,852.00	654.33	151.00	122.16	130.13	126.88	162.48
7,904.00	658.67	152.00	122.81	130.83	127.60	163.55
7,956.00	663.00	153.00	123.46	131.53	128.31	164.63
8,008.00	667.33	154.00	124.11	132.23	129.02	165.70
8,060.00	671.67	155.00	124.76	132.93	129.73	166.78
8,112.00	676.00	156.00	125.41	133.63	130.44	167.86
8,164.00	680.33	157.00	126.06	134.33	131.15	168.93
8,165.04	680.42	157.02	126.07	132.69	131.17	168.95
8,216.00	684.67	158.00	126.71	133.32	131.86	170.01
For each additional			Add			
52.00	4.33	1.00	0.65	0.65	0.71	1.08
104.00	8.67	2.00	1.30	1.30	1.42	2.15
156.00	13.00	3.00	1.95	1.95	2.13	3.23
208.00	17.33	4.00	2.60	2.60	2.85	4.30
260.00	21.67	5.00	3.25	3.25	3.56	5.38
312.00	26.00	6.00	3.90	3.90	4.27	6.46
364.00	30.33	7.00	4.55	4.55	4.98	7.53
416.00	34.67	8.00	5.20	5.20	5.69	8.61
468.00	39.00	9.00	5.85	5.85	6.40	9.68
520.00	43.33	10.00	6.50	6.50	7.12	10.76
10,399.48	866.62	199.99	154.00	160.62	161.74	220.39
10,400.00	866.67	200.00	154.01	160.62	161.75	220.40
For each additional			Add			
52.00	4.33	1.00	0.65	0.65	0.71	1.10
520.00	43.33	10.00	6.50	6.50	7.12	11.02
5,200.00	433.33	100.00	65.00	65.00	71.15	110.20
22,360.00	1,863.33	430.00	303.51	310.12	325.39	473.86
For each additional			Add			
52.00	4.33	1.00	0.75	0.75	0.75	1.10
520.00	43.33	10.00	7.50	7.50	7.50	11.02
5,200.00	433.33	100.00	75.00	75.00	75.00	110.20
27,145.04	2,262.09	522.02	379.24	387.00	394.41	575.27
27,196.00	2,266.33	523.00	374.11	380.73	394.99	576.35

NOTE: This table assumes that the taxpayer
(a) has no allowances against income other than the personal allowance for a single or married person (b) has no benefits-in-kind or deductions from his or her pay other than income tax and nati...
insurance (c) has no deductions from his or her pay (e.g. pension fund contributions) other than income tax and national insurance.

r married woman not liable at reduced rate of national insurance
Liable at reduced rate of national insurance

Take Home Pay: From 6 April 1994: (B) Contracted Out

Left table

GROSS PAY Per Annum Up to £	Per Month £	Per Week £	NET TAKE HOME PAY per week Single Person * £	Married Man £	Married Woman or Widow ** £	COST TO EMPLOYER per week £
,963·48	246·96	56·99	56·99	56·99	56·99	56·99
,964·00	247·00	57·00	55·86	55·86	54·81	59·02
,016·00	251·33	58·00	56·78	56·78	55·77	60·03
,068·00	255·67	59·00	57·70	57·70	56·73	61·03
,120·00	260·00	60·00	58·61	58·61	57·69	62·04
,172·00	264·33	61·00	59·53	59·53	58·65	63·05
,224·00	268·67	62·00	60·45	60·45	59·61	64·05
,276·00	273·00	63·00	61·37	61·37	60·57	65·06
,328·00	277·33	64·00	62·29	62·29	61·54	66·06
,380·00	281·67	65·00	63·20	63·20	62·50	67·07
,432·00	286·00	66·00	64·12	64·12	63·46	68·08
,445·00	287·08	66·25	64·35	64·35	63·70	68·33
,497·00	291·42	67·25	65·07	65·27	64·46	69·33
For each additional			Add			
52·00	4·33	1·00	0·72	0·92	0·76	1·04
104·00	8·67	2·00	1·44	1·84	1·52	2·07
156·00	13·00	3·00	2·15	2·75	2·28	3·11
208·00	17·33	4·00	2·87	3·67	3·05	4·14
260·00	21·67	5·00	3·59	4·59	3·81	5·18
312·00	26·00	6·00	4·31	5·51	4·57	6·22
364·00	30·33	7·00	5·03	6·43	5·33	7·25
416·00	34·67	8·00	5·74	7·34	6·09	8·29
468·00	39·00	9·00	6·46	8·26	6·85	9·32
520·00	43·33	10·00	7·18	9·18	7·62	10·36
,148·00	429·00	99·00	87·87	94·42	88·64	103·25
,165·16	430·43	99·33	88·10	94·72	88·89	103·59
,199·48	433·29	99·99	88·58	95·19	89·39	104·27
,200·00	433·33	100·00	88·58	95·20	89·40	104·28
,252·00	437·67	101·00	89·30	95·92	90·16	105·31
,304·00	442·00	102·00	90·02	96·64	90·92	106·33
,356·00	446·33	103·00	90·74	97·35	91·68	107·36
,408·00	450·67	104·00	91·46	98·07	92·45	108·38
,460·00	455·00	105·00	92·17	98·79	93·21	109·41
,512·00	459·33	106·00	92·89	99·51	93·97	110·44
,564·00	463·67	107·00	93·61	100·23	94·73	111·46
,616·00	468·00	108·00	94·33	100·94	95·49	112·49
,668·00	472·33	109·00	95·05	101·66	96·25	113·51
,720·00	476·67	110·00	95·76	102·38	97·02	114·54
,772·00	481·00	111·00	96·48	103·10	97·78	115·57
,824·00	485·33	112·00	97·20	103·82	98·54	116·59
,876·00	489·67	113·00	97·92	104·53	99·30	117·62
,928·00	494·00	114·00	98·64	105·25	100·06	118·64
,980·00	498·33	115·00	99·35	105·97	100·82	119·67
,032·00	502·67	116·00	100·07	106·69	101·58	120·70
,084·00	507·00	117·00	100·79	107·41	102·35	121·72
,136·00	511·33	118·00	101·51	108·12	103·11	122·75
,188·00	515·67	119·00	102·23	108·84	103·87	123·77
,240·00	520·00	120·00	102·94	109·56	104·63	124·80
,292·00	524·33	121·00	103·66	110·28	105·39	125·83
,344·00	528·67	122·00	104·38	111·00	106·15	126·85
,396·00	533·00	123·00	105·10	111·71	106·91	127·88
,448·00	537·07	123·94	105·77	112·39	107·63	128·84
,448·00	537·33	124·00	105·81	112·43	107·67	128·90

Right table

GROSS PAY Per Annum Up to £	Per Month £	Per Week £	NET TAKE HOME PAY per week Single Person * £	Married Man £	Married Woman or Widow ** £	COST TO EMPLOYER per week £
For each additional			Add			
52·00	4·33	1·00	0·67	0·72	0·71	1·06
104·00	8·67	2·00	1·34	1·44	1·42	2·11
156·00	13·00	3·00	2·00	2·15	2·13	3·17
208·00	17·33	4·00	2·67	2·87	2·85	4·22
260·00	21·67	5·00	3·34	3·59	3·56	5·28
312·00	26·00	6·00	4·01	4·31	4·27	6·34
364·00	30·33	7·00	4·68	5·03	4·98	7·39
416·00	34·67	8·00	5·34	5·74	5·69	8·45
468·00	39·00	9·00	6·01	6·46	6·40	9·50
520·00	43·33	10·00	6·68	7·18	7·12	10·56
7,539·48	628·29	144·99	119·83	127·50	122·61	153·34
7,540·00	628·33	145·00	119·84	127·51	122·61	153·35
7,592·00	632·67	146·00	120·51	128·23	123·33	154·40
7,644·00	637·00	147·00	121·18	128·95	124·04	155·44
7,696·00	641·33	148·00	121·85	129·66	124·75	156·49
7,748·00	645·67	149·00	122·51	130·38	125·46	157·53
7,800·00	650·00	150·00	123·18	131·10	126·17	158·58
7,852·00	654·33	151·00	123·85	131·82	126·88	159·63
7,904·00	658·67	152·00	124·52	132·54	127·60	160·67
7,956·00	663·00	153·00	125·19	133·25	128·31	161·72
8,008·00	667·33	154·00	125·85	133·97	129·02	162·76
8,060·00	671·67	155·00	126·52	134·69	129·73	163·81
8,112·00	676·00	156·00	127·19	135·41	130·44	164·86
8,164·00	680·33	157·00	127·86	136·13	131·15	165·90
8,165·04	680·42	157·02	127·87	136·14	131·17	165·92
8,216·00	684·67	158·00	128·53	135·14	131·86	166·95
For each additional			Add			
52·00	4·33	1·00	0·67	0·67	0·71	1·08
104·00	8·67	2·00	1·34	1·34	1·42	2·15
156·00	13·00	3·00	2·00	2·00	2·13	3·23
208·00	17·33	4·00	2·67	2·67	2·85	4·30
260·00	21·67	5·00	3·34	3·34	3·56	5·38
312·00	26·00	6·00	4·01	4·01	4·27	6·46
364·00	30·33	7·00	4·68	4·68	4·98	7·53
416·00	34·67	8·00	5·34	5·34	5·69	8·61
468·00	39·00	9·00	6·01	6·01	6·40	9·68
520·00	43·33	10·00	6·68	6·68	7·12	10·76
10,399·48	866·62	199·99	156·57	163·19	161·74	216·07
10,400·00	866·67	200·00	156·58	162·20	161·75	216·08
For each additional			Add			
52·00	4·33	1·00	0·67	0·67	0·71	1·10
520·00	43·33	10·00	6·68	6·68	7·12	11·02
5,200·00	433·33	100·00	66·80	66·80	71·15	110·20
22,360·00	1,863·33	430·00	310·22	316·84	325·39	462·64
For each additional			Add			
52·00	4·33	1·00	0·75	0·75	0·75	1·10
520·00	43·33	10·00	7·50	7·50	7·50	11·02
5,200·00	433·33	100·00	75·00	75·00	75·00	110·20
27,145·04	2,262·09	522·02	380·38	387·00	394·41	561·29
27,196·00	2,266·33	523·00	379·82	386·44	394·99	562·34

TE: This table assumes that the taxpayer
(a) has no allowances against income other than the personal allowance for a single or married person (b) has no benefits-in-kind or deductions from his or her pay other than income tax and national insurance (c) has no deductions from his or her pay (e.g. pension fund contributions) other than income tax and national insurance.

17·5%   VAT

Basic Price £ or p	VAT @ 17·5% £ or p	Inclusive Price £ or p	Basic Price £ or p	VAT @ 17·5% £ or p	Inclusive Price £ or p	Basic Price £	VAT @ 17·5% £	Inclusive Price £	Basic Price £	VAT @ 17·5% £	Inclusive Price £	Basic Price £	VAT @ 17·5% £	Inclusive Price £	Basic Price £	VAT @ 17·5% £	Inclusive Price £
1	0·18	1·18	51	8·93	59·93	101	17·68	118·68	151	26·43	177·43	201	35·18	236·18	251	43·93	294·93
2	0·35	2·35	52	9·10	61·10	102	17·85	119·85	152	26·60	178·60	202	35·35	237·35	252	44·10	296·10
3	0·53	3·53	53	9·28	62·28	103	18·03	121·03	153	26·78	179·78	203	35·53	238·53	253	44·28	297·28
4	0·70	4·70	54	9·45	63·45	104	18·20	122·20	154	26·95	180·95	204	35·70	239·70	254	44·45	298·45
5	0·88	5·88	55	9·63	64·63	105	18·38	123·38	155	27·13	182·13	205	35·88	240·88	255	44·63	299·63
6	1·05	7·05	56	9·80	65·80	106	18·55	124·55	156	27·30	183·30	206	36·05	242·05	256	44·80	300·80
7	1·23	8·23	57	9·98	66·98	107	18·73	125·73	157	27·48	184·48	207	36·23	243·23	257	44·98	301·98
8	1·40	9·40	58	10·15	68·15	108	18·90	126·90	158	27·65	185·65	208	36·40	244·40	258	45·15	303·15
9	1·58	10·58	59	10·33	69·33	109	19·08	128·08	159	27·83	186·83	209	36·58	245·58	259	45·33	304·33
10	1·75	11·75	60	10·50	70·50	110	19·25	129·25	160	28·00	188·00	210	36·75	246·75	260	45·50	305·50
11	1·93	12·93	61	10·68	71·68	111	19·43	130·43	161	28·18	189·18	211	36·93	247·93	261	45·68	306·68
12	2·10	14·10	62	10·85	72·85	112	19·60	131·60	162	28·35	190·35	212	37·10	249·10	262	45·85	307·85
13	2·28	15·28	63	11·03	74·03	113	19·78	132·78	163	28·53	191·53	213	37·28	250·28	263	46·03	309·03
14	2·45	16·45	64	11·20	75·20	114	19·95	133·95	164	28·70	192·70	214	37·45	251·45	264	46·20	310·20
15	2·63	17·63	65	11·38	76·38	115	20·13	135·13	165	28·88	193·88	215	37·63	252·63	265	46·38	311·38
16	2·80	18·80	66	11·55	77·55	116	20·30	136·30	166	29·05	195·05	216	37·80	253·80	266	46·55	312·55
17	2·98	19·98	67	11·73	78·73	117	20·48	137·48	167	29·23	196·23	217	37·98	254·98	267	46·73	313·73
18	3·15	21·15	68	11·90	79·90	118	20·65	138·65	168	29·40	197·40	218	38·15	256·15	268	46·90	314·90
19	3·33	22·33	69	12·08	81·08	119	20·83	139·83	169	29·58	198·58	219	38·33	257·33	269	47·08	316·08
20	3·50	23·50	70	12·25	82·25	120	21·00	141·00	170	29·75	199·75	220	38·50	258·50	270	47·25	317·25
21	3·68	24·68	71	12·43	83·43	121	21·18	142·18	171	29·93	200·93	221	38·68	259·68	271	47·43	318·43
22	3·85	25·85	72	12·60	84·60	122	21·35	143·35	172	30·10	202·10	222	38·85	260·85	272	47·60	319·60
23	4·03	27·03	73	12·78	85·78	123	21·53	144·53	173	30·28	203·28	223	39·03	262·03	273	47·78	320·78
24	4·20	28·20	74	12·95	86·95	124	21·70	145·70	174	30·45	204·45	224	39·20	263·20	274	47·95	321·95
25	4·38	29·38	75	13·13	88·13	125	21·88	146·88	175	30·63	205·63	225	39·38	264·38	275	48·13	323·13
26	4·55	30·55	76	13·30	89·30	126	22·05	148·05	176	30·80	206·80	226	39·55	265·55	276	48·30	324·30
27	4·73	31·73	77	13·48	90·48	127	22·23	149·23	177	30·98	207·98	227	39·73	266·73	277	48·48	325·48
28	4·90	32·90	78	13·65	91·65	128	22·40	150·40	178	31·15	209·15	228	39·90	267·90	278	48·65	326·65
29	5·08	34·08	79	13·83	92·83	129	22·58	151·58	179	31·33	210·33	229	40·08	269·08	279	48·83	327·83
30	5·25	35·25	80	14·00	94·00	130	22·75	152·75	180	31·50	211·50	230	40·25	270·25	280	49·00	329·00
31	5·43	36·43	81	14·18	95·18	131	22·93	153·93	181	31·68	212·68	231	40·43	271·43	281	49·18	330·18
32	5·60	37·60	82	14·35	96·35	132	23·10	155·10	182	31·85	213·85	232	40·60	272·60	282	49·35	331·35
33	5·78	38·78	83	14·53	97·53	133	23·28	156·28	183	32·03	215·03	233	40·78	273·78	283	49·53	332·53
34	5·95	39·95	84	14·70	98·70	134	23·45	157·45	184	32·20	216·20	234	40·95	274·95	284	49·70	333·70
35	6·13	41·13	85	14·88	99·88	135	23·63	158·63	185	32·38	217·38	235	41·13	276·13	285	49·88	334·88
36	6·30	42·30	86	15·05	101·05	136	23·80	159·80	186	32·55	218·55	236	41·30	277·30	286	50·05	336·05
37	6·48	43·48	87	15·23	102·23	137	23·98	160·98	187	32·73	219·73	237	41·48	278·48	287	50·23	337·23
38	6·65	44·65	88	15·40	103·40	138	24·15	162·15	188	32·90	220·90	238	41·65	279·65	288	50·40	338·40
39	6·83	45·83	89	15·58	104·58	139	24·33	163·33	189	33·08	222·08	239	41·83	280·83	289	50·58	339·58
40	7·00	47·00	90	15·75	105·75	140	24·50	164·50	190	33·25	223·25	240	42·00	282·00	290	50·75	340·75
41	7·18	48·18	91	15·93	106·93	141	24·68	165·68	191	33·43	224·43	241	42·18	283·18	291	50·93	341·93
42	7·35	49·35	92	16·10	108·10	142	24·85	166·85	192	33·60	225·60	242	42·35	284·35	292	51·10	343·10
43	7·53	50·53	93	16·28	109·28	143	25·03	168·03	193	33·78	226·78	243	42·53	285·53	293	51·28	344·28
44	7·70	51·70	94	16·45	110·45	144	25·20	169·20	194	33·95	227·95	244	42·70	286·70	294	51·45	345·45
45	7·88	52·88	95	16·63	111·63	145	25·38	170·38	195	34·13	229·13	245	42·88	287·88	295	51·63	346·63
46	8·05	54·05	96	16·80	112·80	146	25·55	171·55	196	34·30	230·30	246	43·05	289·05	296	51·80	347·80
47	8·23	55·23	97	16·98	113·98	147	25·73	172·73	197	34·48	231·48	247	43·23	290·23	297	51·98	348·98
48	8·40	56·40	98	17·15	115·15	148	25·90	173·90	198	34·65	232·65	248	43·40	291·40	298	52·15	350·15
49	8·58	57·58	99	17·33	116·33	149	26·08	175·08	199	34·83	233·83	249	43·58	292·58	299	52·33	351·33
50	8·75	58·75	100	17·50	117·50	150	26·25	176·25	200	35·00	235·00	250	43·75	293·75	300	52·50	352·50
500	88	588	600	105	705	700	123	823	800	140	940	900	158	1,058	1,000	175	1,175

VAT Content of Inclusive Prices   17·5%

Incl· Price £ or p	VAT Content @ 17·5% £ or p	Basic Price £ or p	Incl· Price £ or p	VAT Content @ 17·5% £ or p	Basic Price £ or p	Incl· Price £	VAT Content @ 17·5% £	Basic Price £	Incl· Price £	VAT Content @ 17·5% £	Basic Price £	Incl· Price £	VAT Content @ 17·5% £	Basic Price £	Incl· Price £	VAT Content @ 17·5% £	Basic Price £
1	0·15	0·85	51	7·60	43·40	101	15·04	85·96	151	22·49	128·51	201	29·94	171·06	251	37·38	213·62
2	0·30	1·70	52	7·74	44·26	102	15·19	86·81	152	22·64	129·36	202	30·09	171·91	252	37·53	214·47
3	0·45	2·55	53	7·89	45·11	103	15·34	87·66	153	22·79	130·21	203	30·23	172·77	253	37·68	215·32
4	0·60	3·40	54	8·04	45·96	104	15·49	88·51	154	22·94	131·06	204	30·38	173·62	254	37·83	216·17
5	0·74	4·26	55	8·19	46·81	105	15·64	89·36	155	23·09	131·91	205	30·53	174·47	255	37·98	217·02
6	0·89	5·11	56	8·34	47·66	106	15·79	90·21	156	23·23	132·77	206	30·68	175·32	256	38·13	217·87
7	1·04	5·96	57	8·49	48·51	107	15·94	91·06	157	23·38	133·62	207	30·83	176·17	257	38·28	218·72
8	1·19	6·81	58	8·64	49·36	108	16·09	91·91	158	23·53	134·47	208	30·98	177·02	258	38·43	219·57
9	1·34	7·66	59	8·79	50·21	109	16·23	92·77	159	23·68	135·32	209	31·13	177·87	259	38·57	220·43
10	1·49	8·51	60	8·94	51·06	110	16·38	93·62	160	23·83	136·17	210	31·28	178·72	260	38·72	221·28
11	1·64	9·36	61	9·09	51·91	111	16·53	94·47	161	23·98	137·02	211	31·43	179·57	261	38·87	222·13
12	1·79	10·21	62	9·23	52·77	112	16·68	95·32	162	24·13	137·87	212	31·57	180·43	262	39·02	222·98
13	1·94	11·06	63	9·38	53·62	113	16·83	96·17	163	24·28	138·72	213	31·72	181·28	263	39·17	223·83
14	2·09	11·91	64	9·53	54·47	114	16·98	97·02	164	24·43	139·57	214	31·87	182·13	264	39·32	224·68
15	2·23	12·77	65	9·68	55·32	115	17·13	97·87	165	24·57	140·43	215	32·02	182·98	265	39·47	225·53
16	2·38	13·62	66	9·83	56·17	116	17·28	98·72	166	24·72	141·28	216	32·17	183·83	266	39·62	226·38
17	2·53	14·47	67	9·98	57·02	117	17·43	99·57	167	24·87	142·13	217	32·32	184·68	267	39·77	227·23
18	2·68	15·32	68	10·13	57·87	118	17·57	100·43	168	25·02	142·98	218	32·47	185·53	268	39·91	228·09
19	2·83	16·17	69	10·28	58·72	119	17·72	101·28	169	25·17	143·83	219	32·62	186·38	269	40·06	228·94
20	2·98	17·02	70	10·43	59·57	120	17·87	102·13	170	25·32	144·68	220	32·77	187·23	270	40·21	229·79
21	3·13	17·87	71	10·57	60·43	121	18·02	102·98	171	25·47	145·53	221	32·91	188·09	271	40·36	230·64
22	3·28	18·72	72	10·72	61·28	122	18·17	103·83	172	25·62	146·38	222	33·06	188·94	272	40·51	231·49
23	3·43	19·57	73	10·87	62·13	123	18·32	104·68	173	25·77	147·23	223	33·21	189·79	273	40·66	232·34
24	3·57	20·43	74	11·02	62·98	124	18·47	105·53	174	25·91	148·09	224	33·36	190·64	274	40·81	233·19
25	3·72	21·28	75	11·17	63·83	125	18·62	106·38	175	26·06	148·94	225	33·51	191·49	275	40·96	234·04
26	3·87	22·13	76	11·32	64·68	126	18·77	107·23	176	26·21	149·79	226	33·66	192·34	276	41·11	234·89
27	4·02	22·98	77	11·47	65·53	127	18·91	108·09	177	26·36	150·64	227	33·81	193·19	277	41·26	235·74
28	4·17	23·83	78	11·62	66·38	128	19·06	108·94	178	26·51	151·49	228	33·96	194·04	278	41·40	236·60
29	4·32	24·68	79	11·77	67·23	129	19·21	109·79	179	26·66	152·34	229	34·11	194·89	279	41·55	237·45
30	4·47	25·53	80	11·91	68·09	130	19·36	110·64	180	26·81	153·19	230	34·26	195·74	280	41·70	238·30
31	4·62	26·38	81	12·06	68·94	131	19·51	111·49	181	26·96	154·04	231	34·40	196·60	281	41·85	239·15
32	4·77	27·23	82	12·21	69·79	132	19·66	112·34	182	27·11	154·89	232	34·55	197·45	282	42·00	240·00
33	4·91	28·09	83	12·36	70·64	133	19·81	113·19	183	27·26	155·74	233	34·70	198·30	283	42·15	240·85
34	5·06	28·94	84	12·51	71·49	134	19·96	114·04	184	27·40	156·60	234	34·85	199·15	284	42·30	241·70
35	5·21	29·79	85	12·66	72·34	135	20·11	114·89	185	27·55	157·45	235	35·00	200·00	285	42·45	242·55
36	5·36	30·64	86	12·81	73·19	136	20·26	115·74	186	27·70	158·30	236	35·15	200·85	286	42·60	243·40
37	5·51	31·49	87	12·96	74·04	137	20·40	116·60	187	27·85	159·15	237	35·30	201·70	287	42·74	244·26
38	5·66	32·34	88	13·11	74·89	138	20·55	117·45	188	28·00	160·00	238	35·45	202·55	288	42·89	245·11
39	5·81	33·19	89	13·26	75·74	139	20·70	118·30	189	28·15	160·85	239	35·60	203·40	289	43·04	245·96
40	5·96	34·04	90	13·40	76·60	140	20·85	119·15	190	28·30	161·70	240	35·74	204·26	290	43·19	246·81
41	6·11	34·89	91	13·55	77·45	141	21·00	120·00	191	28·45	162·55	241	35·89	205·11	291	43·34	247·66
42	6·26	35·74	92	13·70	78·30	142	21·15	120·85	192	28·60	163·40	242	36·04	205·96	292	43·49	248·51
43	6·40	36·60	93	13·85	79·15	143	21·30	121·70	193	28·74	164·26	243	36·19	206·81	293	43·64	249·36
44	6·55	37·45	94	14·00	80·00	144	21·45	122·55	194	28·89	165·11	244	36·34	207·66	294	43·79	250·21
45	6·70	38·30	95	14·15	80·85	145	21·60	123·40	195	29·04	165·96	245	36·49	208·51	295	43·94	251·06
46	6·85	39·15	96	14·30	81·70	146	21·74	124·26	196	29·19	166·81	246	36·64	209·36	296	44·09	251·91
47	7·00	40·00	97	14·45	82·55	147	21·89	125·11	197	29·34	167·66	247	36·79	210·21	297	44·23	252·77
48	7·15	40·85	98	14·60	83·40	148	22·04	125·96	198	29·49	168·51	248	36·94	211·06	298	44·38	253·62
49	7·30	41·70	99	14·74	84·26	149	22·19	126·81	199	29·64	169·36	249	37·09	211·91	299	44·53	254·47
50	7·45	42·55	100	14·89	85·11	150	22·34	127·66	200	29·79	170·21	250	37·23	212·77	300	44·68	255·32
500	74	426	600	89	511	700	104	596	800	119	681	900	134	766	1,000	149	851

8.0% VAT at Lower Rate

Effective from 1 April 1994 levied on Domestic Fuel until 31 March 1995

Basic Price £ or p	VAT @8.0% £ or p	Inclusive Price £ or p	Basic Price £ or p	VAT @8.0% £ or p	Inclusive Price £ or p	Basic Price £	VAT @8.0% £	Inclusive Price £	Basic Price £	VAT @8.0% £	Inclusive Price £	Basic Price £	VAT @8.0% £	Inclusive Price £	Basic Price £	VAT @8.0% £	Inclusive Price £
1	0·08	1·08	51	4·08	55·08	101	8·08	109·08	151	12·08	163·08	201	16·08	217·08	251	20·08	271·08
2	0·16	2·16	52	4·16	56·16	102	8·16	110·16	152	12·16	164·16	202	16·16	218·16	252	20·16	272·16
3	0·24	3·24	53	4·24	57·24	103	8·24	111·24	153	12·24	165·24	203	16·24	219·24	253	20·24	273·24
4	0·32	4·32	54	4·32	58·32	104	8·32	112·32	154	12·32	166·32	204	16·32	220·32	254	20·32	274·32
5	0·40	5·40	55	4·40	59·40	105	8·40	113·40	155	12·40	167·40	205	16·40	221·40	255	20·40	275·40
6	0·48	6·48	56	4·48	60·48	106	8·48	114·48	156	12·48	168·48	206	16·48	222·48	256	20·48	276·48
7	0·56	7·56	57	4·56	61·56	107	8·56	115·56	157	12·56	169·56	207	16·56	223·56	257	20·56	277·56
8	0·64	8·64	58	4·64	62·64	108	8·64	116·64	158	12·64	170·64	208	16·64	224·64	258	20·64	278·64
9	0·72	9·72	59	4·72	63·72	109	8·72	117·72	159	12·72	171·72	209	16·72	225·72	259	20·72	279·72
10	0·80	10·80	60	4·80	64·80	110	8·80	118·80	160	12·80	172·80	210	16·80	226·80	260	20·80	280·80
11	0·88	11·88	61	4·88	65·88	111	8·88	119·88	161	12·88	173·88	211	16·88	227·88	261	20·88	281·88
12	0·96	12·96	62	4·96	66·96	112	8·96	120·96	162	12·96	174·96	212	16·96	228·96	262	20·96	282·96
13	1·04	14·04	63	5·04	68·04	113	9·04	122·04	163	13·04	176·04	213	17·04	230·04	263	21·04	284·04
14	1·12	15·12	64	5·12	69·12	114	9·12	123·12	164	13·12	177·12	214	17·12	231·12	264	21·12	285·12
15	1·20	16·20	65	5·20	70·20	115	9·20	124·20	165	13·20	178·20	215	17·20	232·20	265	21·20	286·20
16	1·28	17·28	66	5·28	71·28	116	9·28	125·28	166	13·28	179·28	216	17·28	233·28	266	21·28	287·28
17	1·36	18·36	67	5·36	72·36	117	9·36	126·36	167	13·36	180·36	217	17·36	234·36	267	21·36	288·36
18	1·44	19·44	68	5·44	73·44	118	9·44	127·44	168	13·44	181·44	218	17·44	235·44	268	21·44	289·44
19	1·52	20·52	69	5·52	74·52	119	9·52	128·52	169	13·52	182·52	219	17·52	236·52	269	21·52	290·52
20	1·60	21·60	70	5·60	75·60	120	9·60	129·60	170	13·60	183·60	220	17·60	237·60	270	21·60	291·60
21	1·68	22·68	71	5·68	76·68	121	9·68	130·68	171	13·68	184·68	221	17·68	238·68	271	21·68	292·68
22	1·76	23·76	72	5·76	77·76	122	9·76	131·76	172	13·76	185·76	222	17·76	239·76	272	21·76	293·76
23	1·84	24·84	73	5·84	78·84	123	9·84	132·84	173	13·84	186·84	223	17·84	240·84	273	21·84	294·84
24	1·92	25·92	74	5·92	79·92	124	9·92	133·92	174	13·92	187·92	224	17·92	241·92	274	21·92	295·92
25	2·00	27·00	75	6·00	81·00	125	10·00	135·00	175	14·00	189·00	225	18·00	243·00	275	22·00	297·00
26	2·08	28·08	76	6·08	82·08	126	10·08	136·08	176	14·08	190·08	226	18·08	244·08	276	22·08	298·08
27	2·16	29·16	77	6·16	83·16	127	10·16	137·16	177	14·16	191·16	227	18·16	245·16	277	22·16	299·16
28	2·24	30·24	78	6·24	84·24	128	10·24	138·24	178	14·24	192·24	228	18·24	246·24	278	22·24	300·24
29	2·32	31·32	79	6·32	85·32	129	10·32	139·32	179	14·32	193·32	229	18·32	247·32	279	22·32	301·32
30	2·40	32·40	80	6·40	86·40	130	10·40	140·40	180	14·40	194·40	230	18·40	248·40	280	22·40	302·40
31	2·48	33·48	81	6·48	87·48	131	10·48	141·48	181	14·48	195·48	231	18·48	249·48	281	22·48	303·48
32	2·56	34·56	82	6·56	88·56	132	10·56	142·56	182	14·56	196·56	232	18·56	250·56	282	22·56	304·56
33	2·64	35·64	83	6·64	89·64	133	10·64	143·64	183	14·64	197·64	233	18·64	251·64	283	22·64	305·64
34	2·72	36·72	84	6·72	90·72	134	10·72	144·72	184	14·72	198·72	234	18·72	252·72	284	22·72	306·72
35	2·80	37·80	85	6·80	91·80	135	10·80	145·80	185	14·80	199·80	235	18·80	253·80	285	22·80	307·80
36	2·88	38·88	86	6·88	92·88	136	10·88	146·88	186	14·88	200·88	236	18·88	254·88	286	22·88	308·88
37	2·96	39·96	87	6·96	93·96	137	10·96	147·96	187	14·96	201·96	237	18·96	255·96	287	22·96	309·96
38	3·04	41·04	88	7·04	95·04	138	11·04	149·04	188	15·04	203·04	238	19·04	257·04	288	23·04	311·04
39	3·12	42·12	89	7·12	96·12	139	11·12	150·12	189	15·12	204·12	239	19·12	258·12	289	23·12	312·12
40	3·20	43·20	90	7·20	97·20	140	11·20	151·20	190	15·20	205·20	240	19·20	259·20	290	23·20	313·20
41	3·28	44·28	91	7·28	98·28	141	11·28	152·28	191	15·28	206·28	241	19·28	260·28	291	23·28	314·28
42	3·36	45·36	92	7·36	99·36	142	11·36	153·36	192	15·36	207·36	242	19·36	261·36	292	23·36	315·36
43	3·44	46·44	93	7·44	100·44	143	11·44	154·44	193	15·44	208·44	243	19·44	262·44	293	23·44	316·44
44	3·52	47·52	94	7·52	101·52	144	11·52	155·52	194	15·52	209·52	244	19·52	263·52	294	23·52	317·52
45	3·60	48·60	95	7·60	102·60	145	11·60	156·60	195	15·60	210·60	245	19·60	264·60	295	23·60	318·60
46	3·68	49·68	96	7·68	103·68	146	11·68	157·68	196	15·68	211·68	246	19·68	265·68	296	23·68	319·68
47	3·76	50·76	97	7·76	104·76	147	11·76	158·76	197	15·76	212·76	247	19·76	266·76	297	23·76	320·76
48	3·84	51·84	98	7·84	105·84	148	11·84	159·84	198	15·84	213·84	248	19·84	267·84	298	23·84	321·84
49	3·92	52·92	99	7·92	106·92	149	11·92	160·92	199	15·92	214·92	249	19·92	268·92	299	23·92	322·92
50	4·00	54·00	100	8·00	108·00	150	12·00	162·00	200	16·00	216·00	250	20·00	270·00	300	24·00	324·00
500	40	540	600	4	648	700	56	756	800	64	864	900	72	972	1,000	80	1,080

VAT Content of Inclusive Prices 8.0%

Basic Price £ or p	VAT @8.0% £ or p	Inclusive Price £ or p	Basic Price £ or p	VAT @8.0% £ or p	Inclusive Price £ or p	Basic Price £	VAT @8.0% £	Inclusive Price £	Basic Price £	VAT @8.0% £	Inclusive Price £	Basic Price £	VAT @8.0% £	Inclusive Price £	Basic Price £	VAT @8.0% £	Inclusive Price £
1	0.07	0.93	51	3.78	47.22	101	7.48	93.52	151	11.19	139.81	201	14.89	186.11	251	18.59	232.41
2	0.15	1.85	52	3.85	48.15	102	7.56	94.44	152	11.26	140.74	202	14.96	187.04	252	18.67	233.33
3	0.22	2.78	53	3.93	49.07	103	7.63	95.37	153	11.33	141.67	203	15.04	187.96	253	18.74	234.26
4	0.30	3.70	54	4.00	50.00	104	7.70	96.30	154	11.41	142.59	204	15.11	188.89	254	18.81	235.19
5	0.37	4.63	55	4.07	50.93	105	7.78	97.22	155	11.48	143.52	205	15.19	189.81	255	18.89	236.11
6	0.44	5.56	56	4.15	51.85	106	7.85	98.15	156	11.56	144.44	206	15.26	190.74	256	18.96	237.04
7	0.52	6.48	57	4.22	52.78	107	7.93	99.07	157	11.63	145.37	207	15.33	191.67	257	19.04	237.96
8	0.59	7.41	58	4.30	53.70	108	8.00	100.00	158	11.70	146.30	208	15.41	192.59	258	19.11	238.89
9	0.67	8.33	59	4.37	54.63	109	8.07	100.93	159	11.78	147.22	209	15.48	193.52	259	19.19	239.81
10	0.74	9.26	60	4.44	55.56	110	8.15	101.85	160	11.85	148.15	210	15.56	194.44	260	19.26	240.74
11	0.81	10.19	61	4.52	56.48	111	8.22	102.78	161	11.93	149.07	211	15.63	195.37	261	19.33	241.67
12	0.89	11.11	62	4.59	57.41	112	8.30	103.70	162	12.00	150.00	212	15.70	196.30	262	19.41	242.59
13	0.96	12.04	63	4.67	58.33	113	8.37	104.63	163	12.07	150.93	213	15.78	197.22	263	19.48	243.52
14	1.04	12.96	64	4.74	59.26	114	8.44	105.56	164	12.15	151.85	214	15.85	198.15	264	19.56	244.44
15	1.11	13.89	65	4.81	60.19	115	8.52	106.48	165	12.22	152.78	215	15.93	199.07	265	19.63	245.37
16	1.19	14.81	66	4.89	61.11	116	8.59	107.41	166	12.30	153.70	216	16.00	200.00	266	19.70	246.30
17	1.26	15.74	67	4.96	62.04	117	8.67	108.33	167	12.37	154.63	217	16.07	200.93	267	19.78	247.22
18	1.33	16.67	68	5.04	62.96	118	8.74	109.26	168	12.44	155.56	218	16.15	201.85	268	19.85	248.15
19	1.41	17.59	69	5.11	63.89	119	8.81	110.19	169	12.52	156.48	219	16.22	202.78	269	19.93	249.07
20	1.48	18.52	70	5.19	64.81	120	8.89	111.11	170	12.59	157.41	220	16.30	203.70	270	20.00	250.00
21	1.56	19.44	71	5.26	65.74	121	8.96	112.04	171	12.67	158.33	221	16.37	204.63	271	20.07	250.93
22	1.63	20.37	72	5.33	66.67	122	9.04	112.96	172	12.74	159.26	222	16.44	205.56	272	20.15	251.85
23	1.70	21.30	73	5.41	67.59	123	9.11	113.89	173	12.81	160.19	223	16.52	206.48	273	20.22	252.78
24	1.78	22.22	74	5.48	68.52	124	9.19	114.81	174	12.89	161.11	224	16.59	207.41	274	20.30	253.70
25	1.85	23.15	75	5.56	69.44	125	9.26	115.74	175	12.96	162.04	225	16.67	208.33	275	20.37	254.63
26	1.93	24.07	76	5.63	70.37	126	9.33	116.67	176	13.04	162.96	226	16.74	209.26	276	20.44	255.56
27	2.00	25.00	77	5.70	71.30	127	9.41	117.59	177	13.11	163.89	227	16.81	210.19	277	20.52	256.48
28	2.07	25.93	78	5.78	72.22	128	9.48	118.52	178	13.19	164.81	228	16.89	211.11	278	20.59	257.41
29	2.15	26.85	79	5.85	73.15	129	9.56	119.44	179	13.26	165.74	229	16.96	212.04	279	20.67	258.33
30	2.22	27.78	80	5.93	74.07	130	9.63	120.37	180	13.33	166.67	230	17.04	212.96	280	20.74	259.26
31	2.30	28.70	81	6.00	75.00	131	9.70	121.30	181	13.41	167.59	231	17.11	213.89	281	20.81	260.19
32	2.37	29.63	82	6.07	75.93	132	9.78	122.22	182	13.48	168.52	232	17.19	214.81	282	20.89	261.11
33	2.44	30.56	83	6.15	76.85	133	9.85	123.15	183	13.56	169.44	233	17.26	215.74	283	20.96	262.04
34	2.52	31.48	84	6.22	77.78	134	9.93	124.07	184	13.63	170.37	234	17.33	216.67	284	21.04	262.96
35	2.59	32.41	85	6.30	78.70	135	10.00	125.00	185	13.70	171.30	235	17.41	217.59	285	21.11	263.89
36	2.67	33.33	86	6.37	79.63	136	10.07	125.93	186	13.78	172.22	236	17.48	218.52	286	21.19	264.81
37	2.74	34.26	87	6.44	80.56	137	10.15	126.85	187	13.85	173.15	237	17.56	219.44	287	21.26	265.74
38	2.81	35.19	88	6.52	81.48	138	10.22	127.78	188	13.93	174.07	238	17.63	220.37	288	21.33	266.67
39	2.89	36.11	89	6.59	82.41	139	10.30	128.70	189	14.00	175.00	239	17.70	221.30	289	21.41	267.59
40	2.96	37.04	90	6.67	83.33	140	10.37	129.63	190	14.07	175.93	240	17.78	222.22	290	21.48	268.52
41	3.04	37.96	91	6.74	84.26	141	10.44	130.56	191	14.15	176.85	241	17.85	223.15	291	21.56	269.44
42	3.11	38.89	92	6.81	85.19	142	10.52	131.48	192	14.22	177.78	242	17.93	224.07	292	21.63	270.37
43	3.19	39.81	93	6.89	86.11	143	10.59	132.41	193	14.30	178.70	243	18.00	225.00	293	21.70	271.30
44	3.26	40.74	94	6.96	87.04	144	10.67	133.33	194	14.37	179.63	244	18.07	225.93	294	21.78	272.22
45	3.33	41.67	95	7.04	87.96	145	10.74	134.26	195	14.44	180.56	245	18.15	226.85	295	21.85	273.15
46	3.41	42.59	96	7.11	88.89	146	10.81	135.19	196	14.52	181.48	246	18.22	227.78	296	21.93	274.07
47	3.48	43.52	97	7.19	89.81	147	10.89	136.11	197	14.59	182.41	247	18.30	228.70	297	22.00	275.00
48	3.56	44.44	98	7.26	90.74	148	10.96	137.04	198	14.67	183.33	248	18.37	229.63	298	22.07	275.93
49	3.63	45.37	99	7.33	91.67	149	11.04	137.96	199	14.74	184.26	249	18.44	230.56	299	22.15	276.85
50	3.70	46.30	100	7.41	92.59	150	11.11	138.89	200	14.81	185.19	250	18.52	231.48	300	22.22	277.78
500	37	463	600	44	556	700	52	648	800	59	741	900	67	833	1,000	74	926

25% Dividend Tax Credits

from 6 April 1993

Net dividend £ or p	Tax credit £ or p	Net dividend £ or p	Tax credit £ or p	Net dividend £	Tax credit £	Net dividend £	Tax credit £	Net dividend £	Tax credit £	Net dividend £	Tax credit £	Net dividend £	Tax credit £	Net dividend £	Tax credit £	Net dividend £	Tax credit £	Net dividend £	Tax credit £
1	0·25	51	12·75	101	25·25	151	37·75	201	50·25	251	62·75	301	75·25	351	87·75	401	100·25	451	112·75
2	0·50	52	13·00	102	25·50	152	38·00	202	50·50	252	63·00	302	75·50	352	88·00	402	100·50	452	113·00
3	0·75	53	13·25	103	25·75	153	38·25	203	50·75	253	63·25	303	75·75	353	88·25	403	100·75	453	113·25
4	1·00	54	13·50	104	26·00	154	38·50	204	51·00	254	63·50	304	76·00	354	88·50	404	101·00	454	113·50
5	1·25	55	13·75	105	26·25	155	38·75	205	51·25	255	63·75	305	76·25	355	88·75	405	101·25	455	113·75
6	1·50	56	14·00	106	26·50	156	39·00	206	51·50	256	64·00	306	76·50	356	89·00	406	101·50	456	114·00
7	1·75	57	14·25	107	26·75	157	39·25	207	51·75	257	64·25	307	76·75	357	89·25	407	101·75	457	114·25
8	2·00	58	14·50	108	27·00	158	39·50	208	52·00	258	64·50	308	77·00	358	89·50	408	102·00	458	114·50
9	2·25	59	14·75	109	27·25	159	39·75	209	52·25	259	64·75	309	77·25	359	89·75	409	102·25	459	114·75
10	2·50	60	15·00	110	27·50	160	40·00	210	52·50	260	65·00	310	77·50	360	90·00	410	102·50	460	115·00
11	2·75	61	15·25	111	27·75	161	40·25	211	52·75	261	65·25	311	77·75	361	90·25	411	102·75	461	115·25
12	3·00	62	15·50	112	28·00	162	40·50	212	53·00	262	65·50	312	78·00	362	90·50	412	103·00	462	115·50
13	3·25	63	15·75	113	28·25	163	40·75	213	53·25	263	65·75	313	78·25	363	90·75	413	103·25	463	115·75
14	3·50	64	16·00	114	28·50	164	41·00	214	53·50	264	66·00	314	78·50	364	91·00	414	103·50	464	116·00
15	3·75	65	16·25	115	28·75	165	41·25	215	53·75	265	66·25	315	78·75	365	91·25	415	103·75	465	116·25
16	4·00	66	16·50	116	29·00	166	41·50	216	54·00	266	66·50	316	79·00	366	91·50	416	104·00	466	116·50
17	4·25	67	16·75	117	29·25	167	41·75	217	54·25	267	66·75	317	79·25	367	91·75	417	104·25	467	116·75
18	4·50	68	17·00	118	29·50	168	42·00	218	54·50	268	67·00	318	79·50	368	92·00	418	104·50	468	117·00
19	4·75	69	17·25	119	29·75	169	42·25	219	54·75	269	67·25	319	79·75	369	92·25	419	104·75	469	117·25
20	5·00	70	17·50	120	30·00	170	42·50	220	55·00	270	67·50	320	80·00	370	92·50	420	105·00	470	117·50
21	5·25	71	17·75	121	30·25	171	42·75	221	55·25	271	67·75	321	80·25	371	92·75	421	105·25	471	117·75
22	5·50	72	18·00	122	30·50	172	43·00	222	55·50	272	68·00	322	80·50	372	93·00	422	105·50	472	118·00
23	5·75	73	18·25	123	30·75	173	43·25	223	55·75	273	68·25	323	80·75	373	93·25	423	105·75	473	118·25
24	6·00	74	18·50	124	31·00	174	43·50	224	56·00	274	68·50	324	81·00	374	93·50	424	106·00	474	118·50
25	6·25	75	18·75	125	31·25	175	43·75	225	56·25	275	68·75	325	81·25	375	93·75	425	106·25	475	118·75
26	6·50	76	19·00	126	31·50	176	44·00	226	56·50	276	69·00	326	81·50	376	94·00	426	106·50	476	119·00
27	6·75	77	19·25	127	31·75	177	44·25	227	56·75	277	69·25	327	81·75	377	94·25	427	106·75	477	119·25
28	7·00	78	19·50	128	32·00	178	44·50	228	57·00	278	69·50	328	82·00	378	94·50	428	107·00	478	119·50
29	7·25	79	19·75	129	32·25	179	44·75	229	57·25	279	69·75	329	82·25	379	94·75	429	107·25	479	119·75
30	7·50	80	20·00	130	32·50	180	45·00	230	57·50	280	70·00	330	82·50	380	95·00	430	107·50	480	120·00
31	7·75	81	20·25	131	32·75	181	45·25	231	57·75	281	70·25	331	82·75	381	95·25	431	107·75	481	120·25
32	8·00	82	20·50	132	33·00	182	45·50	232	58·00	282	70·50	332	83·00	382	95·50	432	108·00	482	120·50
33	8·25	83	20·75	133	33·25	183	45·75	233	58·25	283	70·75	333	83·25	383	95·75	433	108·25	483	120·75
34	8·50	84	21·00	134	33·50	184	46·00	234	58·50	284	71·00	334	83·50	384	96·00	434	108·50	484	121·00
35	8·75	85	21·25	135	33·75	185	46·25	235	58·75	285	71·25	335	83·75	385	96·25	435	108·75	485	121·25
36	9·00	86	21·50	136	34·00	186	46·50	236	59·00	286	71·50	336	84·00	386	96·50	436	109·00	486	121·50
37	9·25	87	21·75	137	34·25	187	46·75	237	59·25	287	71·75	337	84·25	387	96·75	437	109·25	487	121·75
38	9·50	88	22·00	138	34·50	188	47·00	238	59·50	288	72·00	338	84·50	388	97·00	438	109·50	488	122·00
39	9·75	89	22·25	139	34·75	189	47·25	239	59·75	289	72·25	339	84·75	389	97·25	439	109·75	489	122·25
40	10·00	90	22·50	140	35·00	190	47·50	240	60·00	290	72·50	340	85·00	390	97·50	440	110·00	490	122·50
41	10·25	91	22·75	141	35·25	191	47·75	241	60·25	291	72·75	341	85·25	391	97·75	441	110·25	491	122·75
42	10·50	92	23·00	142	35·50	192	48·00	242	60·50	292	73·00	342	85·50	392	98·00	442	110·50	492	123·00
43	10·75	93	23·25	143	35·75	193	48·25	243	60·75	293	73·25	343	85·75	393	98·25	443	110·75	493	123·25
44	11·00	94	23·50	144	36·00	194	48·50	244	61·00	294	73·50	344	86·00	394	98·50	444	111·00	494	123·50
45	11·25	95	23·75	145	36·25	195	48·75	245	61·25	295	73·75	345	86·25	395	98·75	445	111·25	495	123·75
46	11·50	96	24·00	146	36·50	196	49·00	246	61·50	296	74·00	346	86·50	396	99·00	446	111·50	496	124·00
47	11·75	97	24·25	147	36·75	197	49·25	247	61·75	297	74·25	347	86·75	397	99·25	447	111·75	497	124·25
48	12·00	98	24·50	148	37·00	198	49·50	248	62·00	298	74·50	348	87·00	398	99·50	448	112·00	498	124·50
49	12·25	99	24·75	149	37·25	199	49·75	249	62·25	299	74·75	349	87·25	399	99·75	449	112·25	499	124·75
50	12·50	100	25·00	150	37·50	200	50·00	250	62·50	300	75·00	350	87·50	400	100·00	450	112·50	500	125·00
On **Tax**		£1,000 £250		£1,500 £375		£2,000 £500		£2,500 £625		£3,000 £750		£3,500 £875		£4,000 £1,000		£4,500 £1,125		£5,000 £1,250	